Additional Praise for
Real Reade

C000293020

"Scott Allan's Undefeated rewards with of the wisdom and truths we desire for guidance in our life's journey. I worked for writer and motivational speaker Zig Ziglar helping get his message out to the world. Scott Allan is on a par with Zig and many other top-rated motivators concerned about the productivity, fulfillment, and advancement of mankind. Reading and applying the principles, strategies, and tactics in each page of Undefeated inspires and compels one to rise above adversity and continue in the joy of the journey for its own sake."
— **Undefeated Reader** *Michael Popoviki*

"Have you ever felt like you haven't achieved your dreams or goals? Or perhaps you're simply not happy where your life is heading? Then give Scott Allan's book a read. I am a "firm" believer in never giving up and I have been my entire life. I believe he hits on exactly the essential issues that may get your life moving forward and he's included the steps to help you do it." — **Undefeated Reader**, *Alberta Cotner*

"This is not a book to read and put down. This is a book to read again and again. It is well written in an easy to read style with lots of motivational and inspirational quotes peppered throughout the book. It delves into why we defeat ourselves by not following through on our dreams and ambitions. It identifies the traits of achievers and provides step by step actions on how to develop perseverance and start finishing those things that are important to you. This is the best book I've read this year - it delivers what it says—how to be unstoppable." — **Undefeated Reader,** *Richard D.*

"If you've ever felt like you were stuck, or like something within yourself is holding you back from pursuing your dream, then you need to give this book a read. Scott Allan speaks directly to you in plain, simple language that's easy to understand. He also provides step-by-step action guides to help you achieve your goals, combat your fears, and break bad habits. Whether your dream is to open your own business, run a marathon, or learn how to play an instrument, you'll find inspiration and motivation here." — **Undefeated Reader,** *J.A. Newbery*

"Something resonated with me in every chapter. This got me to take action. Given a practical plan of action. I'm not overwhelmed. My goals are achievable!" — **Undefeated Reader,** *Joanna Barker*

"For the past two years, I felt like everything in my life was going wrong. I felt like a victim of bad circumstances and like the odds were stacked against me. I sat around feeling sorry for myself and hoping things would change and get better all on their own. I'm so thankful for this book because if I didn't read it I'd still be sitting and waiting for a miracle to happen. It taught me that I am not a victim, I am in control of my destiny and if I want things to change then I have to take the initiative and make it happen. This book will give you a step by step guide to making your dreams come true." — **Undefeated Reader,** *Mary Jay*

"The ability to take people out from the clutches of defeat is not an easy task. Every now and then an awesome book comes along and makes that happen. Undefeated I such a book. It offers no illusions that defeat will not happen from time to time. what it does do is teach you to not give up but find better ways to learn and grow from the experiences that life will throw at you from time to time." — **Undefeated Reader,** *Samson Thomas*

"Scott Allan is a master storyteller and motivational author, and this is his best book yet. Engaging, inspiring, and rich with personal experience, Scott identifies the thoughts and behaviors that so commonly get in the way of success and top performance - and provides helpful antidotes to each. Promotes resilience even in the face of adversity. A wise and helpful read." — **Undefeated Reader,** *Steve Wrigley*

"The author goes over the many reasons people are stuck and/or haven't reached their goals. And then gives you the tools to move forward in your life. Make no mistake... This is a fantastic book. It is incredibly inspiring and eye-opening. You can sense how much he cares for the reader, his excitement on sharing his experiences, what he has learned, and wanting to bring this to the world to make other lives better. That is a rarity. This book is a wealth of information that I will tap into over and over again." — **Undefeated Reader,** *Cindy B.*

"My teenager stopped me in my tracks this year when she said, "Mom—another new project, you have so many projects you haven't even finished" Boy, that was a deep cut. So this book is definitely for me. So much of this hit home. (going to the gym – my only reason is because I expect quicker results and when they don't happen, I give up... love chapter 12) I love the 11-Point goal system. Finally, I will be able to get the important things done."
— **Undefeated Reader,** *Susan Abraham*

Undefeated.

By Scott Allan

Books by Scott Allan

Empower Your Thoughts: Control Worry and Anxiety, Develop a Positive Mental Attitude, and Master Your Mindset

Empower Your Fear: Leverage Your Fears To Rise Above Mediocrity and Turn Self-Doubt Into a Confident Plan of Action

Empower Your Success: Success Strategies to Maximize Performance, Take Positive Action, and Engage Your Enthusiasm for Living a Great Life

Rejection Reset: A Strategic Step-By-Step Program for Restoring Self-Confidence, Reshaping an Inferior Mindset, and Thriving In a Shame-Free Lifestyle

Rejection Free: How To Choose Yourself First and Take Charge of Your Life By Confidently Asking For What You Want

Do It Scared: Charge Forward With Confidence, Conquer Resistance, and Break Through Your Limitations

Relaunch Your Life: Break the Cycle of Self-Defeat, Destroy Negative Emotions, and Reclaim Your Personal Power

Drive Your Destiny: Create a Vision for Your Life, Build Better Habits for Wealth and Health, and Unlock Your Inner Greatness

The Discipline of Masters: Destroy Big Obstacles, Master Your Time, Capture Creative Ideas and Become the Leader You Were Born to Be

The Master of Achievement: Conquer Fear and Adversity, Maximize Big Goals, Supercharge Your Success and Develop a Purpose Driven Mindset

Do the Hard Things First: How to Win Over Procrastination and Master the Habit of Doing Difficult Work

UNDEFEATED

Persevere in the Face of Adversity, Master the Art of Never Giving Up, and Always Beat the Odds Stacked Against You

By Scott Allan

Undefeated: Persevere in the Face of Adversity, Master the Art of Never Giving Up, and Always Beat the Odds Stacked Against You
by Scott Allan © 2021

CONTENTS

The Art of Surrender and Defeat 13

Breaking the Barriers of Defeat 23

The 10 Traits of Undefeated Achievers 37

The Cost of Giving Up— Willing vs Unwilling Power Choices 45

Stuck in Limbo Land (& the End of Self-Pity) 53

Building Your Master Goal System 59

The Fears That Force Us Into Defeat 71

Surrender the Addiction to 'Instant Success'.................................... 81

Breaking Through Tough Obstacles...91

Overcoming Bad Habits and the Limitations of Comfort................. 103

The *Achilles Heel* of Self-Defeat (and How to Prevent Getting Caught
Off Guard)..113

Fuel Your Enthusiasm and Do the Work You Love 123

Visualizing the Big Win 131

Rising Up and Rebounding After the Knockdown............................ 139

Maximize Your Energy & Increase Vitality...................................... 149

The Habit of Intentional Action and Deliberate Practice 161

The Unbeatable Mindset: "I Can Do This!".....................................175

Building Your Undefeated Lifestyle 187

About Scott Allan 201

Free Gift: The <u>Fearless Confidence</u> Action Guide

As a way of saying thanks for your purchase, I'm offering a free digital product that's exclusive to readers of the *Empowered Your Success Series*:

The Fearless Confidence Action Guide: 17 Action Plans for Overcoming Fear and Increasing Confidence

To learn more, <u>go to the link</u> below and gain access right now:

<u>https://scottallanauthor.com/fearless-confidence-action-guide/</u>

<u>https://scottallanauthor.com/fearless-confidence-action-guide/</u>

"And once the storm is over, you won't remember how you **made it through**, how you managed to survive. You won't even be sure whether the storm is really over, but one thing is certain: When you come **out of the storm**, you **won't be the same person** who walked in. That's what this storm's all about."

– Haruki Murakami

The Art of Surrender
and Defeat

"Your toughness is made up of equal parts persistence and experience. You don't so much outrun your opponents as outlast and outsmart them, and the toughest opponent of all is the one inside your head."

– Joe Henderson

Do you always start something new but give up too soon out of frustration, boredom, or hopelessness? Are you tired of committing to a goal you can't complete? Do you experience moments of defeat in your life, and now you believe total failure is what you're destined for?

In this book Undefeated, I'll share a system of techniques and strategies that makes you unstoppable. You will learn to crush the weak areas of your life preventing you from moving forward.

You will be able to recognize the hidden obstacles in your life defeating you, and break these barriers down. You will discover how to implement specific tactics to overcome fear paralysis and replace the bad habits killing your potential big wins in life.

If this sounds like something you want, Undefeated is the book for you. This book is designed to be an action guide to keep you moving forward. It is a companion to show you the unlimited possibilities available to you.

The time for waiting is over. The time to take total charge of your life is now.

It doesn't matter what you've lost before, or how badly you failed to measure up in the past. The past does not dictate your future. You can only predict your future by taking intentional action today. The choices you make from here on in tilt the moment in your favor. By focusing in on what matters most, you can eliminate the all the noise of what matters least.

But first . . .

Learning the Art of Self-Defeat

I learned the art of defeat early in life.

For many years, I was a "giver-upper." I had always been great at starting something but struggled to continue after it became too difficult. Losing confidence in being able to finish, I would throw in the towel and start something else. This soon became a trait of mine, and over time, developed into a habit that would impact everything I attempted.

Giving up was what I did best when the going got tough. As a result, I scored low in most things throughout life: Courses at school, employment opportunities, and relationships. I said YES to the easy things in life, and NO to the things that mattered—and I said NO to the things I really wanted!

It's one thing to throw away something you don't need. It's another to give it up, when it's all you can think of, and it means everything to you. You feel that desperation of loss, like this is my thing, and I must have it.

For a long time, I failed to connect with the positive traits needed to make an impact: Confidence, respect, and self-love.

Defeated by character flaws and a system of self-defeating behaviors that seized control of my life, I let these things lead my future. I opted to live a life built on default choices, instead of taking a proactive approach. I defeated myself by just letting life happen and not making it happen.

That all changed when I decided to turn it around. Instead of just accepting life as it was, I made a decision to make it the way I wanted it to be. Instead of being defeated by bad habits and negative thinking patterns, I created a stream of better habits and changed my way of thinking. Instead of living out a system of false beliefs that halted self-growth, I started believing in the "impossibilities" that eventually manifested into my reality.

Everything I once deemed impossible transformed into the life I lead today. If I can do this, so can you. The biggest barrier you face is your own mind, and as you will see later on, the mind is yours to master.

This is why I wrote this book. I want you to become an unstoppable success machine. No matter what story your past is—or the self-imposed limitations feeding negative messages to your mind—you are in control of your destiny.

Destiny is an outcome driven by choice and not by chance.

You can choose to win or lose. You can make the choice to stand out, or stay hidden in the shadows. You decide to stay small or become larger than life.

Better yet, you can still lose everything and come out a winner. The path of the Undefeated warrior is not met with a string of consistent successes, but a long trail of failure.

You can only fail after you stop trying. The path for the Undefeated warrior is a journey in motion. You continue to push forward, fall back, get up again, and push ahead some more. Only one more mile, one more step. Take it as far as you think you can go…and then go just another step further.

Do you have what it takes to accept this challenge and, to embrace this way of life?

You know you do. I know you do.

The time for taking action is now.

Scott Allan: A Brief Intro

My name is Scott Allan. In my books, courses and coaching, I teach people how to handle rejection, dissolve their fear, and build a freedom-rich lifestyle.

By joining me on this journey, you learn how to build and live the life you have always imagined. My mission is to help you discover your true potential by teaching you the system for turning your faraway dreams into a solid reality. By learning the strategies in this book—and paying close attention to your purpose-driven mindset—you will become the ultimate greatness you are seeking.

You see, I believe that **successful living is a series of small actions taken consistently every day** to build a thriving lifestyle. My purpose is to guide you towards taking the necessary actions that bring you closer to achieving your goals and eliminating distractions that keep you stuck.

Like you, I struggle with many of life's ups and downs. Sometimes I lost a few and other times I won. I don't claim to have all the answers but, I will do whatever it takes to go the distance and run that extra mile.

In my years of studying and practicing the strategies leading to mindset mastery, I came across many examples of real people who lost everything. They lost it all, gained it all back, and sometimes lost it all over again. But humans are resilient when tapped into the inner drive that propels them forward.

You have this internal drive that makes you undefeatable. Even if you haven't discovered it yet, it's there, like the flame in the dark waiting to be discovered, waiting for you to awaken and seize the day.

In *Undefeated*, I will show you how to reclaim this power and develop a mindset forged of mental steel to win no matter the odds stacked against you. Nothing is over until you have surrendered and given up completely. And you and I are far from giving up. We're just getting going, because the first lesson is this:

There is no surrender until you decide. You set the rules in this game. You choose to keep going...or not. You know the consequences of giving up and giving in and, you know the rewards for persevering through difficult times.

If you're still with me, you are here to go the distance.

About the Undefeated Journey

In this book, Undefeated, I am going to teach you how to become undefeatable, unbeatable, and live by a superior system of excellence designed to reveal your greatness. You will learn to never give up when faced with heavy opposition, and to always finish what you start.

This system is not about making you great; you already are that greatness. Rather, to shake your consciousness awake so it's aware of how great you truly are. And then, leveraging this greatness for absolute influence.

You are here because you are tired of being defeated; not just by the world around you, but the world within you. Most people are defeated by their own hand, and they don't realize it.

If you are running a marathon, writing a book, or building your business from the ground-up, you will be able to finish what you set out to do. No matter how many times you may fail or screw things up, you will not be defeated until you decide to be. Giving up is a choice, and not a condition in your life.

The game isn't over until you say it is.

I know I've said this already, but the message must be heard more than once and at least one-hundred before it becomes your reality.

We are defeated, not by the conditions surrounding us, but the choices we make in response to present circumstances.

Throughout most of my life, I have struggled to persevere through hard times. I have given up many times, and **procrastination** became a habit I mastered well—but it was a bad habit that did much damage, and I lost a great many opportunities by allowing it to win.

After growing tired of never finishing anything, I set out to find a winning formula that works. I wanted something that would set me up for success, rather than failure. I needed to change the habits, behaviors, and, most of all, the mindset that were dragging me down and keeping me stuck.

I learned if you never finish anything, and you pursue your work, goals, and dreams only halfway, you have not succeeded. We can't cross a bridge that is only half built. In many cases, we will see how finishing what you set out to become is the road to true happiness, fulfillment—and, yes, what we call "success".

What is success? We hear it all the time, but the word is thrown around so much that it's lost its meaning for many. John Wooden, a former American basketball player and head coach at the University of California, defined success as:

> "Success is peace of mind, which is a direct result of self-satisfaction in knowing you made the effort to do your best to become the best that you are capable of becoming."

You can come up with your own definition of what success means to you, but you will know when you have arrived there. People who stick to the *Road Less Traveled* and persevere through whatever it takes will arrive at that place.

You will emerge an Undefeated Champion, a true warrior of mastering the art of perseverance and breaking all resistance.

This book is about becoming the best and striving to be the best you can be. You will learn the habit of persistence, and what it means to form a resilient, unbreakable mindset. Persistence, perseverance, and resilience are three powerful contributors to achieve anything in your life.

> "Many of life's failures are people who did not realize how close they were to success when they gave up."
>
> — **Thomas Edison**, American Inventor

Embracing Your Bigger Life Plan

If you have been living a life of defeat, it is not because of any one event that happened in your life. A defeatist—someone who fails in life, despite their best intentions—is immersed in a world that supports this level of defeat. That is, a set of consistent habits designed to fail; it's a mindset focusing on negative thoughts, trapped in a cycle of memories; or hanging around with the wrong company, who couldn't care less whether you succeed or not.

It's a recipe for defeat.

To start living the Undefeated lifestyle, you must train your mind, body, and attitude to respond differently to problems. As you will see, whatever you want—if you really want it and are willing to do whatever it takes to get it—will be yours. Throughout this book, we will look at the successful achievers who accomplished amazing feats. They achieved because they believed.

Martin Luther King once said:

> "If you can't fly, then run; if you can't run, then walk; if you can't walk, then crawl, but whatever you do, you have to keep moving forward."

Martin Luther King was undefeatable. He went up against some of the toughest opposition in his lifetime... and he remained undefeated until the end.

With each victory, you will get to climb a little higher and move a little more. The race is won by putting one foot in front of the other. It's not won by the person who can run the fastest, because in this race, there is no such thing as placement.

Nobody is competing against you. You are competing against yourself. You must defeat the demon that lives within your consciousness, the negative voices, the self-doubt, and all the placeholders from your past trying to pull you back there.

Your thoughts, choices, actions, and attitude are core contributors to the success or failure you have endured up until now. These key factors continue to play a role in your level of performance and success in everything you do.

As we will see, life throws problems and challenges into our lives, but it is not the problem itself that is the problem; rather, it is how we deal with it. Will you run from it, avoid it, or tackle it head-on?

Ask yourself these questions: Am I tired of being afraid? Do I want to crawl through life feeling deflated and defeated all the time? Or, am I ready to embrace this winning mindset to become unbeatable and undefeatable?

It's time for you to unravel all the lies, self-imposed limitations, and self-defeating thoughts.

It's time to become **Undefeated**.

"When **defeat comes**, accept it as a signal that your plans are not sound, **rebuild** those plans, and **set sail** once more toward your **coveted goal**."

— **Napoleon Hill,** *The Law of Success*

Breaking the Barriers
of Defeat

"When you have a great and difficult task—something perhaps almost impossible—if you only work a little at a time—every day a little—suddenly, the work will finish itself."

— Isak Dinesen

There are many things we stop doing in life. You simply won't continue doing everything forever. At one point in your life, you may have worked out every day, and then gradually, the workouts became less and less, until you stopped altogether.

You could have been working toward a master's degree, and then your kids came along, so you set it aside until you had more time. You started renovating the house in the hopes of selling it on the market for more cash, but with bigger obligations, you only completed half the work.

As you let go of the projects and goals that once mattered, you opted in to take on different challenges—but did you give up on the goals that could have made a difference in your life? You could be looking back on the decisions you made and saying to yourself, "If only I had stuck with it…"

I know that feeling. It is regret, the ultimate tool of self-defeat. It crushes your drive and forces you into the arena of losers. **If you convince yourself the past is your measure of success, you will make more of the same bad decisions**. Gradually, by giving up on the things that matter, we are buying into the model of defeat.

Looking back on the things you stopped doing, there were reasons for not following through: A lack of progress that made you frustrated and bored; you were too busy with other commitments; or, you just lost interest and pursued new ventures.

But, what happens when giving up becomes more of a habit than anything else? If you have a desire to pick up where you left off, or start what you never started, where does that leave you right now?

Moreover, do you know the reasons why you give up on things, like creative hobbies, ambitious goals, or relationships?

Not deciding to stick with your goal until it's completed leaves you open to giving up too soon before success. This way, you never finish anything. Rather, you end up with a long line of unfinished projects and abandoned plans. **Unbuilt bridges** and half-finished homes that remain unlived in. Your dreams all fail to come to fruition because you never cross the finish line.

Keep in mind it takes a strong level of focused concentration and resilience to see goals, projects, and tasks through to the end. We are busy people, so, as much as we would like to accomplish everything and be super-productive, we must be honest with ourselves about what can be achieved. Don't overcommit and take on too much, knowing you will just defeat your efforts in the end when it gets to be too much.

You might have given up on something years ago that you now regret. You might want to come back to it again someday—but it is important to know why you abandoned your passion before it had a chance to grow.

And let it go, now. Forgive yourself for not following through. If it's something that means that much to you, it will return to pick up where you left it. Taking intentional action is what matters. Let go of all the grandiose ideas of fortune and fame. **Take action on the one thing that can change everything.**

There are a lot of things I gave up over the years which I later came to regret. Some of these were:

- Playing tennis. I was a great player and dreamed of becoming a professional.

- Playing guitar. I tried for a couple months and gave it up. To this day, I still have a deep passion for playing music.

- Writing a book. I am writing again now, but for 20 years, I stopped writing, and it haunted me the entire time.

- Grade-10 math. I failed twice and gave up. I thought I couldn't do math, but I later learned I was wrong.

- Exercise. For years, I went to the gym. Then, one day, I just... stopped.

- Creating a financial portfolio. I started many times and never finished one.

- Pursuing work worth doing. Are you doing what you love? If not, why not? Did you give up trying and settle? (More on this later.)

As soon as you know why you are defeated, you will place yourself in a better position to do something about it. Knowing why you failed is as important as recognizing how you failed. Total awareness of what defeats you is like taking your blindfold off—now you can see what has been interfering with all your best efforts.

Understanding all the reasons you quit so quickly can prevent you from throwing in the towel too soon next time. Be aware of the obstacles that interfere with finishing what you set out to do.

We will look at seven obstacles that could be holding you back. Throughout the book, you'll be able to pinpoint the areas in your own life where you tend to give up before succeeding.

6 Barriers to Living an Undefeated Lifestyle

1. Trying to do it alone.

Have you ever tried to do something on your own, and you reached the point where you just couldn't continue? Maybe it was working on a passion project, playing an instrument, writing a book, starting a business, or training for a marathon.

You started out with vigorous enthusiasm, but after several weeks or months, you lost momentum and stopped. It's hard to stay motivated when you don't have anyone cheering you on. It's hard to get the results you expect, as well—which is why I recommend you always look for an accountability partner, or someone you can share the fun with.

You need support. We all do. Having no support is like pushing against gravity and expecting to jump higher than you can. You need a friend, a coach, or a trainer you can dial up when you're on the ropes. When you come up against resistance, it is much easier to get through it with help.

Your chances of quitting decrease significantly when you have someone holding you responsible for finishing. A lack of accountability and support is the #1 reason people stop pursuing their passion.

Don't do this alone. Make the right friends and support yourself with the people who will be there to pull you up when you fall. Even when you are both tired, you can run better when your efforts are combined to reach a result.

2. Get over your excuses.

American author and motivational life coach **Tony Robbins** said:

> "It isn't a lack of resources that is holding us back, but a lack of resourcefulness."

So, the question is: Are there any resources you need access to that would leverage your plan to win?

Often, we think if we had more access to better resources, or if the timing were just right, we could achieve more. So, we wait for these things to show up and waste precious time waiting, when all we need is more resourcefulness.

Right now, do you have a:

- Lack of money? You can always get cash when the need is great.

- Lack of energy? You can generate your own energy by exercising, eating better, and meditating.

- Lack of time? Turn off the TV and get a routine going.

- Lack of education? You don't need education. Grab a book. Take a course. All the information and knowledge is available to you in your pocket.

- Lack of courage? Find a role model and model the actions they take, and the habits they consistently practice.

In a world full of abundance, you have everything you need. Make a list of resources right now that you can tap into.

"I don't have any [time, money, friends]," is an excuse to avoid what you should be doing."

People have built empires from nothing but an idea and some innovation, guts, courage, and a plan.

You probably recognize a few of these names:

- Oprah Winfrey

- Michael Jordan

- Harland David Sanders

- Walt Disney

- Henry Ford

- Sam Walton

- Helen Keller

- J.K. Rowling

- Howard Schultz

- George Soros

- Nikola Tesla

People with nothing—and, seemingly, no resources—managed to climb over the hurdles in front of them and achieve what they wanted when it wasn't readily given to them.

What is Stopping You?

<u>Make a list</u> of your excuses that stop you from pushing forward. Which of the reasons above are holding you back from doing the work you want to do?

Here is a list of my top five excuses that stop me from moving ahead and just doing it:

1. "I have to do.......... first before I get started." [But I never get that first thing done so I never start]

2. "I need to do more research. [6 Months later I am still researching]

3. "I don't feel like doing it right now." [But when tomorrow comes I don't feel like doing it either]

4. "There just isn't enough time in the day." [But I found time to watch TV for 2 hours]

5. "If only other people would leave me alone." [But I continued to check my phone for updates every five minutes looking for attention]

All of these excuses just point back to one thing: a reason to procrastinate further. **There is time to do the things you want to do, but you have to make the time.** You won't always feel like doing the tasks that are challenging. But, if you start working on this task, your state will change and, suddenly, the motivation you think you didn't have kicks in ten minutes later.

It is always best when we live with reasons and not excuses. You can validate your excuses and believe in the power of these lies. Or, build a solid list of values and build a reality around these.

Action creates momentum. You achieve the momentum the moment you apply your thoughts towards doing it.

Excuses are self-defeating. You create them to avoid doing something uncomfortable, risky or challenging. While it feels like you're busy with other stuff, are you really busy or just acting like you are?

Don't let your excuses win. Take charge and push back against the mind when it looks for a short cut.

Now that we have looked at the excuses holding you back, it is time to let those go and start living your life.

3. Expecting faster results.

Boredom comes from a lack of progress, loss of interest, or impatience (e.g., "I want it all right now."). If boredom is the issue, there are things you can do to renew your enthusiasm We will look at this later.

Losing interest in something can happen for several reasons.

You expected quicker results. When you didn't get it, you lost your motivation to continue; or maybe you were expecting to be at Point X, but after years of hard work, you are still stuck at Point C.

By failing to move faster than expected—whether the battle is losing weight, saving money, or building your first business—you feel defeated by your lack of progress. You have thoughts like, "I should be further ahead, moving faster." This can cause us to slip into repeating old patterns.

When you return to an old model that defeated you in the past, it will defeat you in the future, too. You must throw away your old model and build a new one to make room for better strategies.

When you have expectations to be at a certain point, and you are struggling to get there, it may be time to shift your expectations. Look at how far you've come. Where are you now, compared to last year? How about 10 years ago? Without realizing it, you are probably making good progress. **Give yourself recognition for the small**

wins along the way. Small wins always lead to a destiny of your own making.

We are all running our own race. You might be slow, but this isn't a race to see who gets to the finish line first. It is a matter of finishing what you started on your own terms.

If you stick with it and keep pushing forward, you will get there. It isn't about reaching some big goal at the end of your destination. Instead, pay attention to the person you are becoming as you work toward something bigger that really matters.

Ask yourself, "Why am I doing this? What will I become, once I master this technique or accomplish this goal?"

My best question is: "How will I **change my life** by remaining Undefeated, and staying committed to going the distance?"

4. Lacking clarity in your goals.

According to current research, less than 3% of the population has written goals, and less than 1% review and update goals regularly. This means there are a lot of people out there, wandering around and wondering what to do with their lives.

Stuck in jobs they hate or spending too much time on devices that demand more attention, people are absorbing unlimited information that leads to nothing. **A weak goal that lacks clarity has no potential to build momentum.**

Clarity—not confusion—builds your future and leads you towards a destiny of your choice.

For example, a friend of mine recently told me that he wanted more money, but he had no idea how much more he wanted, or even why he wanted it. So, without knowing why or what, he will never get excited to act and make it happen.

Just wanting something doesn't make it a goal. Weak goals lead to weak commitments, but if you have goals that are clear and written-out, it will set you up for the right actions.

You'll always be moving in the right direction if you are following the right blueprint. But it must be your plan, and not the plan someone else has told you to pursue. Remember, it is about progressive growth. If your goals are not focused on growth and moving to a better place in the future than where you are now, you won't be excited to work on them.

What is the right blueprint? How do I know I'm on track? It is having absolute clarity in your mission. You will integrate your action plan with your clear vision of a destination you must reach.

If you believe something is impossible—it will be impossible, until someone else proves it is possible. Be the someone who proves it is possible by trying, starting, and finishing your project or challenge. **It is possible if you believe it is**. The same goes for impossibility. It's always impossible if you doubt yourself to reach your goal or overcome the obstacle.

5. A Depletion of energy and motivation.

Physical and mental exhaustion can hold you back from getting started. Be sure to boost your energy levels by exercising, meditating, or listening to podcasts or inspirational music. Resiliency draws its power from vital energy. So, be sure you are doing what it takes to stay alert, frosty, and focused.

You might be working full-time and trying to build a side business in your spare time. You may get home at night, exhausted. You may wake up late and drive one hour to work. How can you be Undefeated if you feel defeated by exhaustion?

Feeling tired or suffering from exhaustion isn't necessarily an excuse, but it is a roadblock for many people. We have to spend our time with family; we have to be at work by 8:30 AM; and we are expected to do everything else—all while remaining what Scott Allan calls "Undefeated."

For the moment, look at your diet and lifestyle. What do you do when you feel tired? How do you eat? Do you watch a lot of TV or use your phone for hours every night?

You can beat your exhaustion, feel great, get plenty of rest, and still have energy left over to spend with your loved ones. And, crush it in your side business. **Success will not happen overnight, but it will build itself over years of consistent action taken in daily small steps.**

6. A focus on doing too many things.

The only thing worse than doing nothing is doing too much and burning out before you get your wings off the ground. **Over-commitment has the same result as no commitment. Spread yourself too thin, and you will defeat yourself at every turn.**

We want to keep things simple. Instead of doing everything, you will choose your battles wisely. What could you do now that will have a long-term, positive effect on your future?

- You can only focus on one big goal at a time.

- You can only learn one habit at a time.

- You can only perform one task at a time.

A lack of focus means, you are either engaged in something that is exciting, or you are having too many thoughts that lead you to become overwhelmed.

Someone said to me recently, "Every day, I have 10 things on my list of stuff to do. I have to finish all of them."

There are things we have to do, and then, there are things we want to do. There are also tasks we have to do so that we can eventually do the things we want to do. We want to focus on the third option. You don't have to do everything; you just think you do.

This is one of the ways we defeat ourselves, by setting up our days with massive to-do lists and stacks of tasks that rob us of our time. **Multi-tasking is problematic for most people.** A lack of focus means you are either engaged in something that is NOT exciting or you are having to put pressure on yourself to do everything. This mindset leads to anxiety as you rush from one task to the next, only doing half of one and half the other.

The human brain is designed to focus on one thing at a time. Earl Miller, a neuroscientist at the Massachusetts Institute of Technology, notes that our brains "don't do a good job of multitasking." When people think they're working on multiple tasks at the same time, they're actually switching from one task to another very quickly. Every time they do, there is a cognitive cost."

You don't have all the time in the world, so select your tasks that lead to the #1 outcome you want. Spending two hours on email most likely won't get you anywhere. But two hours on sketching out your goals for the next year will.

Disengage Your Self-Defeating Limitations

Right now, you are limiting your potential in ways you cannot see. These limitations come in many forms, and you are not fully aware of how your unlimited potential is being destroyed.

In the shape of buried fears, negative thought patterns, and self-defeating behaviors that limit our scope of achieving anything worthwhile, many people flail through life, defeated by the circumstances and events that appear to control their lives.

We complain about the circumstances in life that aren't right: "Why did she do that to me?" or "What was he thinking?" and "Now, I am in a really bad spot."

"The circumstances aren't right," you say. The people surrounding you are not treating you well. You were rejected by your parents, teachers, and peers while growing up. You have feelings of self-doubt and uncertainty, mixed with low self-esteem.

You are not alone. Everyone has been through these experiences of failure and repeated defeat. It is these circumstances that make us better and push our growth to levels we never imagined. If you choose to let your moments of defeat define you, it can fail you.

Viktor Frankl, an Austrian psychiatrist and Holocaust survivor, said:

> "Everything can be taken from a man but one thing, the last of the human freedoms: To choose one's attitude in any given set of circumstances; to choose one's own way."

Self-imposed limitations are holding you back more than the external circumstances that are thrown at you. The truth you have to embrace is: **You are defeating yourself.**

Other people are not acting the way we want them to? Drop your expectations for how they should be acting. YOU can only focus on how YOU respond to the actions taken by others. Take control of your environment and change perspective. Demand nothing from anyone and drop your expectations.

If the world continues to be in a state of chaos that is impacting your way of life, you can choose your attitude at any given moment. It is the only thing that you have direct control over.

If you are now shaking your head and saying, "Yes, that has happened," this is good. Now you know that, if you can disprove one lie that has been limiting your great potential, you can get rid of all of them. You can break down the house of lies one brick at a time. Whatever your limiting beliefs may be, they are just invisible barriers built to protect and confirm your fear.

It's frightening to suddenly realize many of the thoughts, beliefs, and values you hold onto have been the result of earlier conditioning. It has been the accumulation of environment, family, work, and relationships with the thousands of people you've crossed paths with over the years. Each of them has served to construct your foundation in some way.

Let me tell you something else that can bring you great confidence right now: You are already leading the Undefeated lifestyle. That means you have made it this far in life, and, regardless of how far that is, you have not allowed yourself to be beaten. You aren't here by accident. **You are here to discover the greatest mystery there is: Yourself.**

You are nothing less than the best.

Let's move into the next chapter and learn about...

"The 10 Traits of Undefeated Achievers."

"Defeat is a **state of mind**; no one is ever defeated until defeat has been **accepted as a reality**."

— Bruce Lee

The 10 Traits of Undefeated Achievers

"Success usually comes to those who are too busy to be looking for it."

— Henry David Thoreau

Have you ever wondered what superpowers great achievers have? What makes them so much more productive? How do they get more done than anyone else? How do they stick with their goals until they are finished? How do they find the courage to face impossible odds and come out on top?

The 10 Traits of People Who Develop the Undefeated Way of Living

1. The Undefeated have clear, concise goals in line with their greatest passion.

Undefeated people have clearly-defined goals. They know exactly what they want. This level of clarity drives us to act, no matter what the circumstances are.

With your goals in clear sight, and an actionable plan for how you'll get there, you can turn anything into a positive result with the implementation of an actionable plan.

If you have a goal you can't stop thinking about, if it keeps you awake at night, then you need to act on it. **Turn your obsession into reality by giving it 100% of your attention.**

Tell people about your goal. You have to share this with people. Even if they don't act interested, they will pay attention when the changes in your life become obvious. Instead of asking you, "Are you sure you should be doing this?", people will start asking, "How did you do that?"

What are you most passionate about? What is the one passion that occupies your thoughts continuously? How can you inject this passion into achieving your life's vision right now?

2. The Undefeated have a concrete plan supported by a system of actionable habits.

Anyone—whether in business or sports—who has ever overcome any difficult obstacle or achieved a great accomplishment did so with **a specific plan supported by a clear plan of action.**

You must be clear in your actions and intention. You can have good intentions, but without following through, you will only defeat yourself in the end.

These habits may include eating the right foods to get into better shape. If you are in the habit of eating junk food, but you know you need to change this, then adopt the habit of eating more fruits and vegetables. By implementing consistent habits, you can achieve your goal of losing weight and running a marathon or joining a triathlon.

Begin with your goal and work out the actionable habits you need to make it a reality. High-level achievers—people who get their work done—are using this strategy to win. You cannot be defeated if you have a goal driven by directed action.

3. The Undefeated navigate through insurmountable obstacles along the way.

There will always be something blocking you from moving ahead. These are the obstacles that define who we are. You will learn what you are capable of when you can tackle any problem or challenge and find a solution to get around it. In any business or personal goal, you will be challenged to prove what you are capable of.

This isn't something that should cause fear and hesitation; rather, embrace the chance to be your best and show the world you are here to win. Do you ever see people give up on something because it is "too difficult"? Anything in life worth having will not be easy to get. If it were, everyone would get what they want.

Take a moment and think about the obstacles in your life right now. Do you struggle with any self-defeating behaviors, negative thought patterns, or situations that have to be cleared before you can move forward?

Recognize and identify what could potentially hold you back. Then, identify the one action you can take now—even if it is something small—that will push you to confront and overcome this obstacle. Your thoughts are your inner strength that moves all things.

4. The Undefeated develop the conditioned mindset to finish what they start.

Commitment is the key to winning. Look at someone who sets out with a goal in mind and achieves that goal, years—or even decades—later.

Let's look at Ben, for example, someone who started an online business with his wife a little over 10 years ago. They knew from the start they had to put in a certain number of hours per week to get the business off the ground.

They had the passion, the drive, and a plan to launch the business within one year. By committing to a weekly action plan they set for themselves, they created a system whereby they were each responsible for a specific part of the business.

Commitment means sticking with your dream when faced with hard times. You might go through a financial crisis, you might lose your business partner, or a personal disaster might occur, but the committed mind will transcend all obstacles and find a way to finish the race.

5. The Undefeated can visualize the outcome and push ahead until they get there.

A commitment to your dream, and a strategy to take massive action, are followed by a vision of what you strive to accomplish. Everything in your life—whether it succeeds or fails—can be traced back to the vision you hold for your life, and the environment you desire to create.

No vision means a good chance of failing or ending up in some place you don't want to be, because you followed someone else's plan.

You can begin with the end in mind. Visualize your life at the end, and the level of happiness you will have achieved in your life.

When you visualize the outcome of your plan, your mind works to formulate the necessary actions needed. By consciously visualizing the course of action needed, your mind will formulate the steps necessary to take you there.

By knowing ahead of time what needs to be done to reach your destination, you will build momentum in your actions and enhance your enthusiasm to keep pushing ahead.

"Starting strong is good. Finishing strong is epic."

— Robin Sharma

6. The Undefeated are strategic in their approach to doing the work.

Purpose-driven people are committed to working diligently toward their dreams with actionable intent. They organize all activities, thoughts, and actions toward defining this singleness of purpose. They have an organized plan for achieving everything they set out to do.

The individual with a purpose-driven mind has a list of set, actionable items that must be completed, according to the objectives they are working toward.

This strategic mindset toward work is a defining trait you should develop now. By being strategic, preparing ahead, and utilizing every minute for maximum efficiency, you can work less time and be more productive and more satisfied.

What actions could you take every day that would have a significant impact on your life one month from now? What actions could you start doing tomorrow that would change everything if you continued this course for 90 days? Instead of following someone else's plan for your life, what is a plan you could create in alignment with your passions and objectives?

Let's take an example. If you are building a house, and you want to finish it in three months, how much time would you have to allocate to this project each day?

If you break down all the various projects into tasks and allocate an estimated time frame to each of these tasks, then you can crush each piece of work systematically. Set a mini-goal to achieve just one task a day.

7. The Undefeated have realistic expectations.

As I mentioned in the previous chapter, one of the reasons people are defeated is they have unrealistic expectations for what they can achieve.

Remember what Tony Robbins said: "We overestimate what we can do in a month but underestimate what can be achieved in a year."

You have to be realistic about what is possible when you start working toward a goal. If you decide to run a full marathon, but you can barely make it to the 5k mark, you will have to run for several months and build up to it. This takes time. Likewise, when setting up a business, there is a lot to learn, and you will make mistakes along the way.

So, be prepared for setbacks, as well. Not everything will go according to plan. In fact, most of it won't, so part of having realistic expectations is knowing what you are capable of, and how long your projected goal may take.

People who end up defeated often had expectations that were beyond what was possible. After not meeting their own expectations, they feel deflated and convince themselves they are a complete failure, but that is not the case. They just have to reset their expectations and know that being realistic about what can and should be done is part of the formula.

8. The Undefeated are persistent in the face of defeat.

People committed to the "Undefeated Lifestyle" do not give up, surrender, or give in to failure. They perceive failure as a necessary pathway to a successful outcome. Failure is the road to success.

Persistence plays a vital role in succeeding at anything you have a desire to accomplish. For successful people, facing that failure and overcoming their fears to break through obstacles is the only path to winning.

What obstacles do you face now? Are these barriers going to stop you from living your life as it could be lived?

Look at an obstacle in your life that is slowing your progress and map out a list of solutions you can apply today to begin working through it.

Take the best solution and put it into action. If it doesn't work, try another solution. Keep working on this, until you have overcome this surmountable barrier. Often, most obstacles that defeat you are bigger in your mind than they really are.

9. The Undefeated have a superior belief system.

Successful people have unshakable faith in what they can achieve; they believe in their mission, ideas, and importance of purpose. Regardless of obstacles or challenges, they are confident that anything can be overcome, if they believe it can be. They have the foundational belief that they will succeed, overcome any obstacle, and do anything to see the outcome they desire come to fruition.

Most people set limits on themselves because of limiting beliefs. They create limited income, decide they have limited abilities, and create limited learning skills.

However, successful people are limitless in their pursuits. They continue to grow, expand, develop, and reach out to breach the horizons untouched by the masses.

What do you believe in? Do you believe success is a matter of luck or chance? Or, do you believe that anything can happen if you believe in the possibilities? Your beliefs—like your habits—forge a **powerful alliance with destiny**.

10. The Undefeated form unbreakable habits most people avoid.

Albert E.N. Gray, author of the New Common Denominator of Success, said:

> "Successful people are successful because they form the habits of doing those things that failures don't like to do."

This is the most defining characteristic that separates people who do what they love to do from those who do what they are made to do by others.

People who do things most people are afraid of live life as an expression of the choices they have made. Your actions define you. Do what needs to be done for as long as it takes, and you will have very little competition.

Is there an action you have been avoiding because you're afraid of failing, or the road appears to be too difficult, so you procrastinate? Remember, whatever your purpose in this life may be, you will have a much better chance to live life your way when you do things most people would turn away from.

Right now, make a short list of three actions you can take this week that will have a major impact on your performance. Then, from that list of three actions, choose only one action. Focus on this one thing for 30 days. Make this action the key to pushing your momentum to its peak.

"I like things to **happen**, and if they don't happen, I like to **make** them happen."

— Winston Churchill

The Cost of Giving Up—
Willing vs Unwilling Power
Choices

*"Success seems to be largely a matter of hanging on
after others have let go."*

— **William Feather, American author**

Do you have any regrets about the things you never finished? Do you still have unfinished projects on your to-do list? Do you want to change something in your life, but you are still negotiating with yourself? Are you unwilling to give up this but not that?

When I labeled myself as "a person who gets things done", I had to take an honest look at the projects I still had on my incomplete list. What's more, the emotional baggage I invested in unfinished work was having an impact on my mental state. I was always distracted by things that were left abandoned. I had invested years in procrastination and telling myself, "I'll get to it someday," but, ultimately, someday turned into a very long time.

There is a price to pay for giving up the things you love. In some cases, you are saying NO to something that could potentially change your life, but how will you know if you never complete anything? Before you give up so easily, consider the impact it may have on your life. Is this something you can let go of easily? Or, will it still follow you for years—or decades—to come?

I told you earlier I stopped writing for 20 years, but for those 20 years, it grated on me that I had stopped doing the only thing I really wanted to succeed at. It took years of doing work I had little interest in before I pulled the trigger and said, "That's it! I am tired of sitting on my gift." You have to want it more than anything else.

Ask yourself: *By giving up on your only dream, what are you replacing it with?* More television or Instagram Reels? Be careful when you throw in the towel. When you say NO to something, you are saying YES to something else. Are you saying YES to an action that could steal you away from pursuing your one definitive purpose?

Now, this isn't to say we can do everything. That isn't possible, and this book isn't meant to make you feel guilty for stopping what has come to a natural end. But what about the hobbies that bring you pleasure, such as the time you spend working on something that has an impact on your life and the lives of others? The gift you're holding onto could be what the world needs at this time.

There is a cost for giving up and taking the easy way out. For years, I walked this path. **By surrendering to and settling for mediocrity, you are choosing to live a life that is far less than the extraordinary lifestyle it could be.**

Most people I talk to fail, not from making decisions that didn't work out or taking Path A when they should have taken Path B, but, by having no game plan at all. They didn't see the cost involved in giving up what they truly wanted to be, have, and do.

You have to project yourself into the future and visualize what is at stake. What will the outcome be if you don't follow through? How will you feel one year from now if your vision comes to life? Where will you be in five years?

I want you to imagine turning your impossible dream into a reality. Visualize in every detail how this life will look and feel.

It comes down to steady willingness. What are you willing to do to see your work through to the end? What are you committed to working on for as long as it takes to achieve your goal?

If you want to compete in a triathlon, how much training are you willing to put in each week? If you want to write that book, how many words are you willing to pump out every day for the next six months, until you've finished that first draft? If you want to lose weight, how committed are you to ending your daily junk-food habit?

What new habits are you willing to commit to right now?

As we know, most of our projects never get done because we lack the vision to see them finished, but if you can visualize it happening, you can have it in the future.

There is nothing holding you back, except for a lack of vision and willingness to do whatever it takes to finish what you started.

Weighing the Costs of Choosing Defeat

I mentioned earlier that everybody is responsible—to a large degree—for becoming defeated, but this doesn't mean we are failures.

Your ability to succeed or fail boils down to two factors:

1. **Willingness**: What you are willing to do or put up with to succeed in life?

2. **Unwillingness**: What you are unwilling to do or put up with?

> "Spectacular achievement is always preceded by unspectacular preparation."
>
> — Robert Schuller

Willingness Transcends Obstacles

Many of our so-called "problems" in life can be solved easily, if we are more willing to do what it takes to work toward solutions.

Now, here is another side of the story: You may be willing to do what it takes to get to where you want to be, but what are you unwilling to put up with?

You want to start up a business, so you can quit your day job that is stealing your soul, but are you willing to put in the long hours after the regular 9-5 is over? Will you get up at 5am every morning for the next 90 days to get in that extra hour on your one thing?

What are you unwilling to tolerate in your day job? Is it your boss, or your coworkers? Knowing what you are unwilling to put up with strengthens your resolve to make a solid decision.

For example, "I am unwilling to work in this job for another year, so I am committing to working ten hours a week outside my regular job to start my business."

Are you stuck in a relationship that is going nowhere? Is the other person dragging you down?

Turn your thoughts to your unwillingness to tolerate this relationship any longer. Be willing to find a way out, and then exercise that action right away.

In every major shift you experience in your life, it most likely happens because one day, you came to the realization, "I can't tolerate this anymore. I am no longer willing to put up with this. So, I'll do whatever it takes to change it."

People who are unhappy in their jobs, marriages, or financial situations stay there because they are willing to continue suffering to avoid change. I know that sounds like a crazy way to live but look around you at all the suffering going on.

There are people who destroy their health, lose opportunity, and derail themselves at every corner. In many people's lives, where someone is defeated by the lifestyle that they are leading, they blame someone or something:

- "It is the company's fault I am unhappy at work."

- "It is my wife's fault I am so unhappy at home."

- "It is my children's fault I fail as a parent."

- "It is the bank's fault I owe all this money. If only they hadn't sent me that last credit card—even though I was already in debt."

By embracing the attitude that the world is flawed, and we are so right, we make ourselves a victim. Every time you decide something or someone else is in charge of your destiny, your finances, or your life, you become a tool that can be used by anyone.

You have to end this way of thinking right now. By buying into the lie that the world is responsible for your lack of success, you make yourself a weak pawn. You stay stuck in your own mess because you just threw away the tools needed to dig yourself out of a bad place.

Now, think about the things in your life you want to be different. Make a list right now. Just three things will do. Then, ask yourself: What are you willing to do to change it?

Are you willing to give up television? Are you willing to stay up later at night and wake up earlier? Are you willing to change your thoughts so that you develop a positive mindset that moves the needle toward a successful outcome?

Now, what are you unwilling to put up with? Your unwillingness can have as much of an impact as your willingness.

Say to yourself: "I am unwilling to feel like this anymore, so from now on, I am going to..."

What will you do?

It's like this: You have to be honest with yourself. No more negotiating. Are you willing to do this but not that? Are you willing to stop eating fast food to lose weight, but you still want donuts?

You are choosing the life you live at every moment. You are always the master of your destiny. You can decide right now if you want to win, or you will let yourself be defeated. If so, hold onto your excuses and continue to use them. Keep using words that disempower you. Go complain to someone about how wronged you have been, instead of taking relentless action.

Give up the need to be right. Surrender your reluctance to be different. Then, embrace the power of your free will. It is the key to your freedom. This is a powerful revelation. Just knowing your thoughts, actions, and attitude are all within your control can change your life completely.

Still waiting for something to give you permission to pivot? Let me break the suspense. The wait is over. You are the best chance you'll ever have.

No matter what is going on in your life, how bad it is, how much you stand to lose, or the fear that is screaming for some normalcy, you can be yourself in any situation. You are not responsible for the stuff going on—and, in many cases, we become observers, as life goes on around us—but what you can do is choose your response. You can choose to act or not act, or you can choose to just let it go.

However, you don't have to quit your job or become rich to be happy. If these are things you really want, that is fine—go get them—but many simply want greater control over their lives. They want to feel as if they are driving their destiny, instead of being driven by it.

This means tapping into the confidence buried beneath all the self-doubt and the lack of certainty. By choosing not to live your life one way, you are inadvertently deciding to live it in a different way. This is extremely empowering when you make intentional choices.

How My Friend Beat the Drink

A good friend of mine had a problem with drinking from a young age. He came from a family of alcoholics, and he started drinking heavily by the time he was eighteen. He tried to quit for several years but failed. He spent years, defeated by drinking, until finally, he decided he was through suffering.

For years, he negotiated with his consciousness: "Maybe I can drink on the weekends only, or I'll just slow down after three drinks and walk away." He realized to succeed and change his life for the better—because it couldn't get worse—he had to stop bargaining with his addiction and do anything it took to turn it around.

Suddenly, he adapted the mindset of someone willing to do whatever it takes to succeed. He found a mentor—a "sponsor"—who gave him specific instructions on how to succeed.

My friend stayed the course, and he had a ritual every morning. When he got up, he would review a list of actions he was willing to take to stay on course. He also had a list of actions he would not take part in.

Several years later, he was married to someone special, doing work he loved, and, to this day, he remains unwilling to return to the way of life that tried to take everything from him.

Now, this story might be extreme, but you can apply it to your own life. Up until now, is there some area of your life that is defeating you? Have you tried to change it before, but you couldn't? Are you bargaining for your right to continue acting the same way but expecting a different result?

You must be willing to do whatever it takes to shift your mindset, actions, and behavior. You must be willing to throw away the self-imposed limitations. Remember, we are limiting ourselves on a massive scale. Once you can fully accept this, there is nobody else to blame. People who are playing the blame game are not in control of destiny. They are victims of circumstances and remain trapped.

Your willingness is a gift. I encourage you to embrace it and put it into action. You can defeat any limitation, and you can overcome all the obstacles that, at one time in your life, seemed insurmountable.

"Be of good cheer. Do not think of today's failures but of the **success that may come tomorrow**. You have set yourself a **difficult task**, but you will succeed if you **persevere**, and you will find a joy in **overcoming obstacles**."

— Helen Keller

Stuck in Limbo Land
(& the End of Self-Pity)

"One of the greatest discoveries a man makes, one of his great surprises, is to find he can do what he was afraid he couldn't do."

— Henry Ford,
Founder of the *Ford Motor Company*

Recently, I was watching the movie Fight Club. If you have seen the movie, then you remember this scene: Tyler Durden, played by Brad Pitt, pulls a man out of a convenience store, holds a gun to his head, and threatens to kill him if he doesn't start pursuing his dream of becoming a veterinarian—today.

Reluctantly, the man agrees, vowing to quit his job that day and end the life of redundancy he has been living. It's just a movie, but in real life, too, there are many people who wouldn't act on their dreams unless they were forced into it.

How often do we complain about the dreariness of life, only to wake up each day and continue to do the same thing we don't want to do? Doesn't it feel like you are trapped in a vortex of hell when you feel compelled to do something you don't believe in? Are you the person who needs someone to put a gun to their head before they realize time is running out, and the time to act is now?

Nobody has to put a gun to your head to get you to go to work, but what if you had to do something really risky that involved getting really uncomfortable? Would you do it? Could you leave your job to pursue a new life? Could you move to another city or country? What risk would be involved? What would you give up by not doing this?

In other words, stop asking yourself what could happen if you fail in pursuit of your dreams. Instead, ask yourself, "What are the consequences if I don't pursue my gift? What is the risk by staying stuck where I am?"

The path that leads to self-defeat always begins with you. Your choices, decisions, and willingness to push forward are the deciding factors that create your future. Destiny is made, and not a preordained event. You create it as you go. You are creating it right now. You are defeating your sense of purpose by not pursuing a passionate goal that can change everything.

You may be stuck right now, trapped in a rut or a place you believe is the endgame. You are living out a routine that is boring but, at the same time, comfortable. It is boring because it is comfortable, and you think that you're safe, but—like the convenience store clerk in Fight Club, while he inwardly desired to pursue another career he has wanted his whole life—you're stuck in Limbo Land.

Limbo Land is where your **dreams die**.

This is the place for people who are defeated but not dead. They just hang around in there, killing time, watching life as it slowly drifts away. When you kill time doing work that has no impact, and living a life without purpose, you die a little every day.

People trapped in Limbo Land complain about the situation they are trapped in. They gripe about their lack of money and opportunities. They have excuses for never getting ahead. They play the victim card and give false proof of how life has dealt them a bad hand. Limbo Land is a place of suffering.

When you exist to not exist, and you dream of what could have been, you are no longer building a life that can be. You are stuck remembering a life that could have been, and you end up creating a life that will never be.

The ultimate defeat in life is not the race or the battle we lost. It is the race we never took part in, and the battles we never fought.

You have powers within you that have yet to be discovered. There is a greatness just waiting to be unleashed, if only you would stand up and get serious about the limited life you have remaining. Do not waste one more day dreaming about a life you'll never have. Build the life you can have. You will always rise to the level of achievement you hold yourself accountable to.

It is time to cut Limbo Land free and build new territory.

Waiting for circumstances to change your life isn't taking control; rather, it is giving up your right to exercise positive action. When you wait for your world to change, nothing happens, and nothing changes.

The world is in a constant state of flux and shifts radically from one moment to the next. If you are along for the ride, waiting for the shift to pivot your life, you become a hostage to circumstances created by someone or something else.

The events controlled by external forces become the catalyst to control your fate. You condemn the circumstances in your life and complain there is nothing you can do. By taking this path, you are choosing to be defeated.

Here is the secret to breaking out of this passive frame of mind: Own your reality. Know the truth. Everything that has happened to you or is going to happen to you or has happened up until this stage of your life is yours. Own it now. Imagine the power you wield by choosing to own the day. It is yours.

What are you going to do to turn it into a day of victory? Are you going to gripe about the limitations of life or get up and take control of the unlimited opportunities? People who complain about what they lack are coming from a place of scarcity.

Throw away the excuses of self-pity and get out of Limbo Land.

Self-defeat—whether it be in your personal or professional life—is owned by you. Get over the pity. Stop the blaming. Put an end to the complaining. Gut up and do something about it.

Here are the pity excuses we often hear:

- "I've tried to lose weight, and I can't. I'm just not disciplined enough. The online course I bought on weight loss is no good.

I guess I'll go back to my usual diet. At least, I was happier eating."

- "I've tried to start three different businesses, and they failed.

- "I just don't have a knack for this thing. If only the market would stabilize, I could get ahead."

- "Nobody likes me. I don't make friends easily, and I'm always getting rejected. I'm better off alone, anyway."

- "Life isn't fair."

- "I wish there were more opportunities out there."

Here is what I say: No one said life was supposed to be fair. Opportunity is made and rarely an event that happens by coincidence. The pity train is over. Put the brakes on and get off. We need to give ourselves a shake-off and stand up taller than ever before.

This limited way of life ends today. Actions and commitment to forward progress make you who you are.

As I said at the beginning of this book: You are the only person who can be held accountable for your success or failure.

It isn't the fault of the economy, the current global situation, or your past disappointments and failures. These do not define you. Only your actions and commitment to forward progress makes you who you are. You are the model of everything you stand for. Your values are the principles by which the foundations of your life is built on.

You are ready for something that is going to take the world by storm. You know the only person who can make that difference in your life is you. It's time to wake up to the **driving force of your life within you**.

We were not all treated equally or given the proper attention, love, and respect we needed. If that were you, buying into your own pity train continues the cycle of defeat and failure. By acting like you have been defeated already, you are setting the bar low. If you have no plan for your destiny, rest assured—someone else does.

Self-pity is a choice. It is your secret way of giving up. By choosing defeat, you become defeated. Your default becomes a habit of pity. People who are stuck in a rut might blame the world around them for keeping them in this situation, but it isn't the truth.

So, speak the truth right now. Be completely honest with who you are, and why you are here. More importantly, decide how you are going to overcome your internal state of defeat. Will you allow negative internal voices to keep you down? Will your critics be your biggest fans and stop you from trying again? Are you ready to give up and live life without a plan, absent of any passion or plan to win?

The path of the Undefeated rests in your ability to plan, shape, and do something. Therefore, we need big goals to lift us up and put life back in a positive perspective. We need to build momentum that moves us forward and doesn't push us back.

There is no reason to look back on past failures, unless you want to repeat the same mistakes. Don't dwell on past defeats that can't be corrected; rather, learn from your personal defeat and plan for a different approach next time.

My greatest belief is this: If you don't have a plan for your life, somebody else does. If you don't make your own plan of action, you'll be leading someone else's plan.

You will know what it means to be defeated by your own hand if you do nothing to make your situation better or improve your life somehow. By taking massive action and getting out there and doing it, you carve the path for living Undefeated.

In the next chapter, I will teach you my 11-point goal-setting system. By implementing the strategies in this section, you will have a complete goal portfolio up and running within a couple of hours.

"Never confuse a single defeat with a final defeat."

— F. Scott Fitzgerald

Building Your Master Goal System

"What you get by achieving your goals is not as important as what you become by achieving your goals."

— Zig Ziglar

In this chapter, I will walk you through my simple system for creating a goal portfolio, as well as the process for taking action towards achieving your goals. By defining what you want, we can move the needle closer to obtaining it.

Setting Up Your Big Wins

You need a set of passionate goals—and the right actions working together with your goals—to win. If your goals are not setting you on fire, you will fail to follow through and complete them. As soon as you hit your first big roadblock, the temptation to give up will be too strong.

In other words, your goal has to be a passionate undertaking. It has to be big enough to scare you, and something you absolutely must have. After all, why would you spend time pursuing something you don't want?

This might be you right now. You have been pursuing the wrong goals, and you realize if you don't turn things around, you could find yourself giving up and accepting defeat as your outcome.

Now, I'll give you the 11-point goal system I use to remain Undefeated and get things done.

The 11-Point Goal System for Undefeated People

Identify your three Master Goals.

Knowing precisely what you want is the first step to making it happen. Once you set your sights on a target, you commit your goals on paper by writing them down and making it real. Then, you will design a plan for success to take you through to the ultimate outcome.

For the next 10 minutes, write down your three most important goals. Don't worry about the details, or how you are going to achieve these goals. Make three points and identify your big goals. Chances are, you know what they are—even if you have never really identified them before. This is the beginning of clarifying what is important to you.

Action task: Write down your three big goals.

Write it all down.

For the next 30 minutes, take each of these three goals and write down everything you've always wanted to have, do, be, and experience in your lifetime. Don't worry about how crazy it sounds. If it scares you, that's even better.

At this stage, don't think about how you'll accomplish these things. You will feel uncertain and doubt your ability to accomplish your big goals, but that is part of the process.

To create goals that inspire and motivate, they have to be bigger than anything you've tried before. Begin thinking about what you'd like to aim for. On paper, write down where you'd like to go, the skills you want to master, what you want to learn, who you want to meet, and what you desire to build and create.

Action task: Make a list of all the things you've always dreamed of but could never find the time, energy, or motivation to do. Write for as long as you can and create a list of everything you can visualize doing.

Attach a timeframe to your Master Goals.

A deadline reminds you something requires your immediate attention. Without a deadline, you are leaving the door open for procrastination—and believe me, it will come in and take over your life, if you let it. Once you affix a deadline to your goals, they become more real than you could possibly imagine.

No matter how far into the future your dream is, always attach a deadline. A workable timeframe is the anchor that holds the goal in place. Without it, your dreams and enthusiasm will drift away.

A deadline solidifies your commitment and keeps you motivated and inspired. The deadline is your fixed position. Without it, a goal becomes something you hope you'll get around to eventually.

Action task: Attach a completion date to your goals.

Create an action task list for each goal.

A goal without action becomes just a dream or a wish. We need massive action to move our goals forward and start momentum.

For each goal, make a list of actions you can take. This doesn't have to be a complete list. Write down the first action you can take right now to get started.

Smaller goals contribute to the overall completion of a larger goal. These are sub-goals. Your plan of action will involve many steps that lead to the success of each goal. These steps for success may include research, making phone calls, or sending out applications.

In basic terms, your plan is like a to-do list. It is a list of step-by-step tasks to achieve your goal. By breaking down the steps for each goal, you can manage the time allocated to making progress towards each one.

Action task: Write down a set of action steps for each goal. Post these action steps in a visible place.

Visualize the success of your goals.

If you are to create the life and results you desire, develop a practice of imagining and visualizing yourself as already being a success. How do you feel? What has changed in your life? How different do you feel as a person? How did you grow and change by achieving your goals?

From professional sports to the executive boardroom, every successful achievement is made possible, if there is a vision to build it.

Think of your success as having already happened, and your subconscious mind will bridge the gap between the two worlds of the present and what is yet to come. ,

Action task: Spend 10 minutes in the morning and 10 minutes in the evening visualizing your goals.

Get accountability for your goals.

This could be an accountability partner or a group of people who can support you on your journey. Mastermind groups can be very helpful in this case.

For years, I struggled to hit my goals. I failed at deadlines most of the time and didn't enjoy the process of goal-setting but finding an accountability partner changed all that. An accountability partner or support group can hold you accountable in so many ways. For example, your accountability partner or mastermind group can:

- Check in on your progress once a week

- Send daily reminders of the master tasks you are working on for the day or week

- Help you celebrate when you reach the goal that has taken you weeks, months, or years to achieve; and

- Provide solutions to help you break through tough obstacles

Accountability is a great way to stay on track and motivated when you are stuck in procrastination mode, and it gives you the opportunity to talk to someone about your objectives. Find an accountability partner to work with, and you will not only hit your most important goals, but you'll enjoy the process so much more.

Successful people who remain Undefeated are those who can network and create successful teams of people who are willing to support each other.

Action task: Identify the people who can help you with your goals. Then, ask yourself, "How can we help each other succeed?" Look for these people, and when you find them, build your mastermind team of Undefeated warriors.

Identify your #1 Master Goal.

You have identified the three goals you feel most passionate about. From that short list, identify the one goal that means the most to you. It is the one thing, above all else, you desire to have. This should be easy because chances are, you already know what it is. The other two goals are important, but you will want to focus here on one goal first.

It is the one goal that will impact your life in substantial ways. This is designed to break you out of your mold and make the unimaginable come true. It is everything you have ever dreamed of doing and becoming.

Your #1 Master Goal has to be the one thing in life you have always desired the most. It is your grandest adventure, a seemingly insurmountable obstacle that scares you as much as it excites you. It brings everything in your life into direct alignment with the great purpose that governs all things.

Action task: Write down your #1 Master Goal. Why is this your biggest goal? How will it impact your life and the lives of others when it is realized?

Expand on action tasks for Master Goal #1.

The final step is to break each action task into smaller steps, so they are easier to tackle. By breaking them down, you are giving yourself manageable chunks to work with, while reducing stress.

By breaking down the goal into sizeable chunks, it will be easier to track your success.

These smaller steps could include making phone calls, arranging a meeting, or doing research on a subject.

Expand on the action tasks for your #1 goal. Go back to the mind-mapping strategy and write down as many tasks as you can think of—even if they are months away.

Action task: Make a list of action tasks for your #1 Master Goal.

Organize your plan into priority action steps.

Now that you have your list of action tasks, put these in order of importance. What needs to be done today? This week? Within the next three months?

Take five minutes every night before bedtime to write down the one task you will complete the following day. This is a powerful habit. By doing one thing every day, it pushes your goal closer to the finish line.

Taking massive action really means acting consistently, so every day, you must do something that moves the needle.

Action task: Prioritize your action steps.

Identify the barriers blocking your progress.

As with anything, there will be challenges and obstacles to work through. Identify three immediate challenges you will encounter while working towards your goals. This usually comes down to one of three things—or, it could be all three:

1. You lack information. Is there anything you need to know to move ahead? Do you need to take a course, do an interview, or call somebody?

2. A lack of resources. You might need something such as money to continue your goal, but remember, you are limited not by resources but a lack of resourcefulness. This means you can find a way to make it work and get more money. Maybe you need to convince someone to help you, such as a mentor or coach.

3. Your values are confused. There are times when our values are not in alignment with the goals we are pursuing. This requires us to evaluate the values driving us.

Whatever barriers are in our way, there is a way to get through it. Work out the solutions and create an action plan to chip away at the weaknesses.

Action task: Identify the barriers that could hold you back.

Review Your Progress

This is probably the most vital step to effectively manage your goal portfolio. By reviewing your goals on a regular basis, you can easily recognize and monitor your progress. During the review process, you will:

- Identify pending obstacles blocking your path;

- Review and update your action checklist of tasks required to achieve your goal(s):

- Assess your progress and consider whether your deadline is manageable; and

- Add any new thoughts or ideas to support your continued progress.

It is easy to get pulled away from the work you really want to do, but most of our distractions can be managed easily. The reason is most distractions are self-created. Of course, you will always have family situations come up, or a friend drop by who needs something. This is where blocking off time each day to get your work done and put time into your project is critical.

One major distraction many people have is negative or fragmented thinking. Our mind wants to do one thing, while our will wants to do another.

This is when concentration comes into play. When you concentrate on something, you make it your most important priority. You focus your energy on the task, and then concentrate to make sure it is done correctly, and you are doing only those things required to move closer to your goals.

Action task: Review the progress you are making once a week. Take note of the areas in which you are failing and try to tighten them up.

Goal Builder's Checklist

☐ Commit your goal to paper. Write a brief statement about the goal.

☐ Create a working list of steps necessary to achieve this goal.

☐ Visualize the goal coming true.

☐ Create a deadline.

☐ Place the goal into a category.

☐ Define the desired result(s) of achieving your goals.

☐ Monitor and track your progress.

☐ Review your progress.

☐ Revise your goals on a regular basis.

☐ Describe the expected life impact of achieving your goals.

☐ Describe who you will become after achieving a lifelong goal of significant importance.

Tiny Milestones and Celebrating Small Achievements

Goals can be deceiving. You might have goals for yourself, but are they too big? Do you feel overwhelmed when you look over your goals, thinking, "How am I going to do this?" I know how you feel. My goals are big as well, and while there is nothing wrong with shooting for the moon, we can get frustrated if we are working on the same thing a year from now and feel as if we are getting nowhere.

Progress is measured best when it is in small chunks. This means setting small goalposts for yourself that are easy to measure.

Take this book, for example. When I started writing it, I knew it would be about 50K words. That is a lot of writing. Feeling pressured to get it done in two months, I broke it down into chapters, and these are broken down into subheadings. Now I had smaller but manageable goals for each day.

At the end of the day, I could tick off whether I had finished a certain word count or not. Building small milestones into your projects, hobbies, or work is a sure-fire way to stay on track. Every day you are working on this is a day closer to your goal.

I'll give you another example: When I started working out again, I had a goal to be able to do 50 push-ups in one session. That is a lot. So, I started out by doing just five the first day. Then, every day after that, I increased the push-ups by just one. Yes, only one—but after two weeks, I was doing 20 a day. After a month, I was able to do 35-40.

I would have given up without this mini-milestone formula, but by increasing your performance by just 1%, you can make tremendous gains over time. You will hit your target and finish what you set out to do.

How do you set up tiny milestones? Take your goal and break it into the smallest chunks possible. Even if it seems ridiculously tiny, this is better than doing nothing. A 1% improvement is better than 0% any day. If you do nothing, you get nothing, but do one small action, and within two or three weeks, you will see the results you made. If you have been in the habit of giving up on things you love in the past, this could be prevented from now on, if you do the smallest thing possible.

Here is another example: Playing the guitar. Did you know that most of the best songs were created with just three chords? If you spent 80% of your time mastering these three chords, you could play a lot of music.

One of the better reasons small goals work is they remove the overwhelming thought that we must know everything about our passion, if we want to be good at it.

If this were the case, you'd quit after a few months. It takes a lifetime to master anything. That goes for writing books or playing music or sports. We can always be better at something—no matter how good we already are.

Jerry Seinfeld—one of the greatest comedians of our time—still does stand-up comedy to stay sharp. He has $700M and isn't doing it for the money. He remembers when he was a struggling comedian, and how important it was to stay on top of his game.

The tiny milestone strategy is so basic that many people overlook it. They think they have to do more, know everything, and do it perfectly before they can consider themselves to be experts. I'll tell you how to stop giving up on everything: Do a little bit each day. Set your mini-goal for the week. Then, keep hitting that mini-goal each day.

If you focus on developing tiny milestones, here is what you could get done in six months:

- If you write 300 words a day, you'll have written a book;

- Practice the major three chords on a guitar, and you'll be playing songs at parties; and

- Save $5 a day instead of going to Starbucks, and you'll have $1,825 saved in the bank within the first year.

I know lots of people (myself included) who gave up on saving money. They said it was too difficult to keep money in the bank, but they were giving up on the wrong thing. Instead of giving up daily trips to the coffee shop or buying crap they didn't need, they made a decision that saving was difficult and threw in the towel. They continued those habits, throwing away thousands of dollars a year.

However, another friend gave up a few habits, decided achieving his goal of saving $5K a year was more important, and sacked away $400 a month for 12 months. How? Saving a tiny amount every day. Just like you can play an instrument or learn a language by taking it in tiny sessions a day, you can save money, lose weight, or learn a new language, too.

Tiny milestones are easy to manage. You are much less likely to give up on something if you can see your progress happening daily.

Setting up your tiny milestones is easy, too. I'll walk you through a simple, step-by-step process:

1. Write down your #1 goal. Is it losing weight? Writing a book? Decluttering your apartment?

2. Make a list of action steps for each of your tiny milestones. This should only be three for each milestone.

3. Review your progress every week. Do this at the end of the week.

4. Celebrate your big win. Too often, we take goals for granted. You don't have to achieve something amazing to earn your right to celebrate. Every small task completed is a step toward reaching your outcome.

5. Focus on the action and not the overall big picture. In other words, if your goal is to run a marathon, you will have to run often to condition yourself. So just run a few kilometers at a time—or, just one kilometer at a time, if that is all you can handle.

Build these tiny milestones into your daily habits. The consistency of our actions gets us where we want to be.

"Our goals can only be reached through a **vehicle of a plan** in which we must fervently believe and upon which we must **vigorously act**. There is no other route to success."

— **Pablo Picasso**

The Fears That Force Us Into Defeat

"Do the thing you fear to do and keep on doing it…that is the quickest and surest way ever yet discovered to conquer fear."

— **Dale Carnegie**

Your fear is the biggest obstacle in your life today. When fear rules our minds, it sets everything up to fall like dominoes. But, fear doesn't have to be the dominating factor in your life.

Think about this for a moment: What if you could empower your fear to work for you, instead of sabotaging your efforts? What if fear could be used to fuel your greatest gift, instead of killing it?

How many times a day do you tell yourself you can't do something because you are afraid to just get out there and do it? Can you imagine where you would be if you just **do it scared**, no matter what your fear is? Remember this: You are creating fear in your own mind. It is made from your thoughts and beliefs. It is a reaction to imagining the worst-case scenario happening to you.

Your ability to conquer your fear is about putting an end to your mind's madness. Where do you think fear is living all the time? It is only in your mind.

As a coach and author, I speak to people all the time who ask that big question: "How can I stop being afraid?"

Your fear isn't the problem. The illusion we buy into is that fear is in charge. But the truth is, you are in charge of your choices. You determine the mindset that empowers your thoughts. You can choose to let fear win.

When you believe in your fears more than you believe in your ability to handle anything, you are in survival mode. At the first sign of risk or the slight chance of failure, you are ready to flee the scene.

We know if we set out to challenge anything new, we will be afraid from time to time. This is the fear of failure, or the worry that you might get a different result than you expected.

What if my plans don't work out? What will I do if I find out my fear is all-empowering?

The only time you truly lose is when you finally decide to give up.

Why do people give up so easily? Why do we choose to let our fears defeat us? What if we could stick it out for just a while longer, what then?

The Fear of Uncertainty

We know nothing is guaranteed in this life. There is no guarantee of our health or future employment. We don't know if we will become successful within the next five years, or twenty. When you catch yourself having disruptive thoughts and worrying about the future, this will invite fear into your mind. You are giving fear direct permission to take over.

This fear talks to you in self-defeating ways. It breaks down your walls of confidence. You start to make up things in your mind that "might" happen.

It sounds like this:

- "You shouldn't do that. You remember what happened last time?"

- "Wouldn't it be better to watch, instead of participating?"

- "Why are you trying to fix something, if it isn't broken?"

- "You tried before, and it didn't work out. Giving it a second shot will just mean you'll fail twice."

Uncertainty is a lack of trust in yourself and, the way you believe events are designed to turn out. When we live in a state of fear of the future, we are not setting ourselves up for success; we are setting ourselves up for failure. We are sending the universe a message: "I'm scared about things not working out for me, and I need some kind of reassurance."

However, as we already know, there are no guarantees or promises to be made, and just because things are good now doesn't mean they will be good later. In fact, they might be worse, and this makes us more fearful. We think, "If things get worse, how will I survive? What will become of my job and my children?"

A Faith Unbroken

You must develop an unbreakable faith in yourself. You must feed your mindset positive messages. You must know that no matter what happens—if the stock market crashes, a family member gets sick, your pet dies, or you lose your job—you can handle it.

In the end, it is not the situation that creates fear; rather, it is how you perceive the situation.

No matter what, you can take it. No matter what, you will make it and find a way. No matter what, you will not become defeated by the forces working against you. No matter what, this day belongs to you.

Hope for the best but be prepared for the worst. This is the way to ensure you are never defeated. We become upset and panic when bad news happens, because we never see it coming. We never know what is going to happen. That's just the way it is.

Now, what fears are defeating you these days? What do you worry about? How do you deal with rejection at work? Are you worried about being laid off? Are you afraid you might get sick? Do you worry about not having money? Or, do you worry about actually succeeding?

Make a list of the fears you have. Get to know them well. Write them down on paper. I find writing these things down really helps make them real. It takes away the power fear holds over you by revealing what it is, and in which area of your life it exists.

Then, ask yourself how realistic it is that any of this would happen. On a scale of 1-10, how likely is it that your greatest fear is going to happen?

Next, assuming it does happen, could you handle it? Once again, on a scale of 1-10, rate your ability to handle this event. If your score is below 6, you have something to work on. This doesn't mean you will know exactly what to do when the time comes, but at least you'll have faith in the belief that you can handle it. You will find a way.

The Fear of Rejection

This is a topic I know something about, and I am sure you do, too. The fear of rejection defeats everyone at some point in their lives. We all experience it: Rejection in relationships, at the office, and within our own families.

Rejection is a powerful fear. For years, I allowed it to hold me back from pursuing my greatest passion. I didn't want to find out I was no good at the one thing I wanted to do: Writing. So, for years, I would write in secret, as if being found out would bring that rejection to the surface. I was ashamed: If my words were rejected, what would I have left?

In relationships, rejection played a role in everything. There was the fear of the other person finding out I was worthless and rejecting me because I wasn't good enough to be with. Because of the power I allowed rejection to have over me, I lived in defeat for years.

Your fear of rejection has the power to stop you from taking action when you should. This is what I call "rejection avoidance". To avoid being rejected, we reject ourselves before anyone else has a chance to. You stop yourself from going after what you want.

You can't be rejected if you don't take a risk. By avoiding risk, we stay below the radar. Nobody can reject you if they can't see you, but nobody will discover you, either. You will always be a shadow that moves amongst the living.

Is that how you want to exist?

Living in fear of rejection and trying to avoid it means we end up with nothing that we really want. You never get the job you wanted, you never meet the people you could have spent a lifetime with, and you never push your potential to see what you could really do.

You end up defeated and broken.

Unless...

You turn it around. Tackle your rejection head-on. When you are scared, do something about it. When you feel yourself pulling back, recognize you are feeding into your fear and giving it power over you.

Rejection is a sign you're scared because you have more growing to do. When you push yourself beyond your comfort zone, it is scary, isn't it? The first time, yes—but then, you keep doing it. You keep putting yourself out there. Think about the people you could help by writing a book, or the gift of love you could share with someone, if they really got to know you.

What would you do right now if it could be absolutely anything? Are you ashamed of putting yourself out there and taking a chance?

Imagine how happy people would be to meet you, or the lives you could change by writing a book or creating art. Or, just becoming their friend and being a positive influence in their life.

Rejection is largely at work in your imagination. None of it is real. It only has as much power as you choose to give it.

Desensitize the fear of rejection by doing what scares you today. Rejection is not the problem. It is your belief that you are not a person who is worthy of having the things you want in your life. You couldn't be more wrong!

I have coached and worked with hundreds of people with rejection issues. They all said the same thing after recovering: "I had no idea 90% of my rejection issues were created by me." The fear of rejection is the biggest mind trick we play on ourselves.

Am I saying rejection doesn't exist? No—we do get rejected. We fail at times. We get told NO, and then, we get told we aren't good enough, but what matters isn't the rejection itself. It is how you perceive the rejection.

Will you let it defeat you? Or, will you get up and decide right now to give it your best shot by becoming an Undefeated champion in the fight against rejection?

Here are two actions you can try:

1. Get rejected on purpose.

Take a situation that really frightens you and put yourself in a position where the potential for being rejected is high. This will eventually make you immune to rejection—or, at least, this will make it hurt much less.

A friend of mine did this with dating. Once, he was afraid to even speak to a woman, so he set a goal to approach five people a day and ask them out, and, in doing so, he ended up meeting the woman of his dreams. So, you see, breaking past rejection can have a life-changing impact.

Jia Jiang, the author of *Rejection Proof* and owner of RejectionTherapy.com, undertook a massive project in 2012 when he challenged himself to 100 days of Rejection Therapy.

Jia's goal was to desensitize himself to the pain of rejection and overcome his fears. Jia Jiang then set out to conquer his fears by attempting to get rejected through 100 approaches.

Some of the outrageous rejection attempts included:

- Challenge a CEO to a staring contest

- Get a free room at a hotel

- Be the worst salesman possible

- Ask strangers to rate my look

- Trim my hair at PetSmart

You can view all the videos here at 100 Days of Rejection Therapy.

2. Ask for something you want.

When was the last time you asked for something you really wanted? How many times have you hesitated, and then backed down from asking?

Most people who fail do so because they never state what they want from anyone. They are afraid of being judged and rejected, and then failing, so they stay silent and suffer in that silence.

Meanwhile, someone new to the company will walk into the manager's office and get an extra week off in the summer because he asked for it. You need to ask for things that can make your life better. Only you know what those are. Ask, and you might get rejected, but don't ask, and you will certainly end up rejecting yourself.

> "There are two types of people who will tell you that you cannot make a difference in this world: Those who are afraid to try, and those who are afraid you will succeed."
>
> — Ray Goforth

The Fear of Failure

Failing can induce stress and it makes us question our worth and competency. We experience deep fears, driven by anxiety. Failure—and the fear it creates—is persuasive and manipulative. We become convinced we have no chance, so we leave all risk on the table and opt for the easy way out.

People who struggle with a failure mindset have been subjected to:

- Harsh criticism;

- Rejection issues;

- Perfectionistic ideals;

- Unrealistic expectations;

- Humiliating moments;

- A lack of belief in themselves and from others; and

- A lack of love from childhood and personal relationships.

When we are made to believe we are worthless, it creates deeper feelings of defectiveness. Then, we carry this feeling of defectiveness into every aspect of our lives.

We develop a self-defeating mindset that we are never good enough, no matter what we do, and failing is an expectation we learn to live with.

When we fail, it validates all the reasons we are no good, but here's the truth: Nobody is born a failure. It happens after years of negative conditioning. We are trained to fear failure and conditioned to fear change. By resisting failure in life, you are choosing to escape. Our avoidance strategies keep us stuck in a perpetual loop of self-defeat.

Not only do we fear failure, but we walk around with the belief that we're not good enough. We work hard, play hard, and take life very seriously, so as not to let our guard down. We have this ongoing feeling of shame, as if we are embarrassed to be ourselves and would rather be someone else instead.

Failure does not have to be a permanent condition. You might not succeed at what you are striving for today, but eventually—if you stick to it and keep working at it with a driven passion—you'll look back someday with gratitude for the lesson that the struggle taught you.

Before we go any further, I want you to make a failure list. Write down all the things you feel you have failed at, such as relationships, jobs, or anything at which you think you failed to meet your expectations for yourself or others.

Here is my short list:

1. Failed Grade-10 math twice.

2. Failed at starting my own business four times.

3. Failed my driving test three times.

4. Failed at many relationships.

5. Failed to graduate from high school with the rest of my class. (Later, I had to take online classes to pass).

Fail forward. Fail often.

When we fail at something, the first instinct is to pull back, reassess, and then maybe try again—but many people don't try again. They reassess, and then try something less risky, thereby taking another predictable path that is hoped to guarantee success. You will not fail this way, but you won't succeed, either.

The only way forward is to embrace the lessons you learned and go with it. In fact, the people who fail the most get the most. They get ahead, and they get what they have always wanted. The rest are fighting for scraps because they have one thing in common: They are afraid to take massive action and fail forward.

Your defeat is a stepping stone. You can only step up after you've taken three steps back.

"Fear keeps us focused on the past or worried about the future. If we can acknowledge our fear, we can realize that right now, we are okay. Right now, today, we are still alive, and our bodies are working marvelously. Our eyes can still see the beautiful sky. Our ears can still hear the voices of our loved ones."

— **Thich Nhat Hanh**, bestselling author of *Fear*

Surrender the Addiction to 'Instant Success'

"The journey is never-ending. There's always gonna be growth, improvement, adversity; you just gotta take it all in and do what's right, continue to grow, continue to live in the moment."

— Antonio Brown

In today's world, we live in an age where we can get almost anything in a moment. Information, cash, sex, credit, and an endless amount of data can be found anywhere with a quick two-second Google search.

If you want something, you buy it on credit. Need more sugar? Go to the supermarket. Need an energy boost? Try one of those "healthy" energy drinks.

We are living in an "instant, already done for you" society. When it comes to focusing and getting down to working on our passion and toward a better way of life, we lose track of what really matters, as our attention is flipped from one idea to the next. One moment, we are doing this, and the next, we are doing that. We can jump through millions of pieces of data and not remember any of it by the end of the day.

One of the big reasons many people fail in their lives today and are experiencing feelings of defeat is, they have a difficult time staying fixed on any one thing. What this means is you never make progress in any area of your life; rather, you take a piece from here, and a piece from there, and then try to make sense of it all. In the end, you're just left with bits and pieces that never match up.

We are becoming conditioned to expect instant results. You send an email and expect a reply that same afternoon. You get that new job and demand a promotion by the end of the month. You blow through a course online and expect immediate change so you can get on with the next thing.

We are defeated by our own inventions. They are powered to make our lives easier, and although they certainly do, the basics of life have been forgotten. In our rush to get it all right now, we are not focusing on mastering any one area of life. Rather, we are cross-jumping to everything, throwing information together and expecting to build a vehicle for success.

This is all a short-term fix, but a company whose model is based on short-term success finds itself gradually failing. If you are focused on short-term wins, you don't commit to long-term goals, so you fail to build anything sustainable.

When it comes to plugging in your winning formula, bringing back the principle of a long-term, fixed focus is a necessity. Times will change; technology will develop, but if you stay true to your long-term vision and work toward your goals with consistent action, you will build a success that lasts a very long time. Short-term wins are soon forgotten.

We get used to hearing about people who made it big at a young age, the overnight success of someone who just came out of nowhere and is taking the world by storm. The people with seemingly "gifted" talent who make it look easy, and by observing this miracle in others, we see less of it in ourselves.

You might be asking yourself, "Why aren't I that lucky? Why wasn't I born with that gift? What am I doing wrong that I should be doing better?"

When you beat yourself up for not being good enough, and not measuring up to your own expectations, you begin to believe in the "instant success" syndrome. If you have been working on something for years—a business, your health, or a new way of life—and you haven't had much success at it yet, this can be frustrating to hear yourself say.

Impatience is what causes suffering. We beat ourselves up and think, "Why does he get all the breaks? I've been working 12–15 hours a day for the past year, and I am still not there yet."

We all run our own race. There are people out there who create an app and become billionaires a week later. Someone else writes a book, and they get a book deal. A young sports athlete gets drafted right out of high school and goes on to play for a big-league team.

We have instant success all around us, but we fail if we expect it to happen. We hear the stories of others making it, and we want to join the winners, but, in most cases, all we see is the final outcome. The big WIN.

If you want to know how someone became the fastest runner in the world, look at what they did in the years leading up to that success. What training routine did they practice each day? What were they eating (and not eating) to stay in shape? What did they have to sacrifice in order to win?

It may appear that success is served up on a silver platter, but it is a result of the long-term focus and commitment to hitting small goals every day, every week, and every year.

George R.R. Martin, the Game of Thrones creator, is enjoying loads of success now. But before his books became international sensations fueled by the wildly popular TV series, Martin spent years writing his fantasy saga, starting the writing in 1991 and publishing in 1996.

The legendary Kentucky Fried Chicken entrepreneur Colonel Sanders had his recipe rejected about 1000 times. He would spend years in odd jobs, almost going bankrupt, sleeping in his car, before making it years later and selling the franchise at the age of 72.

John Paul Dejoria used to work as a tow truck driver and janitor just to pay the bills. After meeting Paul Mitchell while working at a hair care company, they started a company with a $700 loan. This became known as John Paul Mitchell Systems, a multi-billion-dollar company that produces professional hair care products.

George Soros once made $1 billion dollars in a single day back in the 1990s after shorting the British pound. But years before his sensational rise to fortune, Soros was a teenager living in Hungary when he fled to England to avoid Nazi persecution. Once there, he got educated by first attending the London School of Economics and onwards to earn his degree. After moving to the United States, George Soros worked for a number of big firms as an investment banker. He then started his own hedge fund, building his own company from scratch.

The strategy you need is to build success brick by brick. You don't construct a new home in a day; rather, you build it piece by piece. Each brick stands alone, as an important part of the overall construction. A life is built the same way: Brick by brick; one action at a time; one small victory leads to the next win.

Build Your Vision into Reality

You need a plan for your overall vision. You have to show up with a set of blueprints, so the vision can be built into a reality. Impatience is par for the course. When you feel the need to run ahead before you're ready, remind yourself the journey is the story you will tell.

It is not about reaching a destination that doesn't exist. There is no final outcome. There is only what you can do today to move your needle ahead. You can never be defeated in this life by sticking with your plan, being willing to make mistakes, and changing the direction of your plan when necessary.

> "The future belongs to those who see possibilities before they become obvious."
>
> — John Scully

There are times when we have to be patient—despite wanting everything right now.

I understand the impatience. Maybe you are stuck in a job you want to quit, or you feel frustrated after putting in months or years of work and getting nowhere. You may feel defeated and like you need to start things over again. This can be a good thing, but it can also be a warning sign that you want a fast fix to your situation.

A friend of mine who is a writer decided he wanted to write full-time. But to do that, he had to spend more time writing while juggling a full-time job, his family, and other obligations with his local community and church. He tried hard to keep everything in balance without sacrificing one for the other.

Over time, by working on his writing day-by-day and hitting those smaller goals, he saved enough money for a year's worth of living expenses, and then, when the time was right, he made the leap and quit.

It pays to plan and focus on long-term growth. It reduces your risk of becoming defeated later. It is tempting to want it all today and jump before you're ready. But while we sometimes have to act quickly—even before we are ready—if you are forced into pushing ahead before the time is right, you should take a step back and view your situation from 30,000 feet.

See the whole picture as it is. Are there any areas that could bring you down if they collapse? Can you accept the risk if you fail? Can you afford to be defeated once, and what would that look like? Are you looking for a quick win but not focusing on the whole picture?

Four Steps to Develop Perseverance

Abraham Lincoln once said, "I am a slow walker, but I never walk back."

You might be tired of waiting for fortune to strike, but that doesn't mean you need to stand still and wait for it to happen. Slow progress is still moving forward.

It is not who wins the race but, whether you finish the race at all. Many people never finish the race because they give up if they aren't the first to cross the finish line.

Here are four steps you can implement right now to ensure you stay true to your course with slow, steady action that builds your success over time. Every goal is reached through taking consistent action. This could be massive action or slow, steady strides.

1. Continue adding pieces to your plan.

It takes time to arrive at your goal. In fact, most achievements we hear about are the result of thousands of small actions taken over months, years, or even decades.

By adding a small piece to your plan every day, just by doing one thing, you can have massive results a year from now. Imagine a drop of water is added to a bucket once per hour for 30 days. At the end of those 30 days, you will have a full bucket.

Adding to your plan is critical, but so is revising the parts of your strategy that are not working anymore. Is there any part of your work you can delegate to free up more time?

If you are overwhelmed by doing too much, look to outsourcing to move the needle and get more done without stressing out.

The more dominoes you can knock down, the greater your confidence will grow, and you will continue to move ahead—even if it is just one step a day.

2. Focus on long-term growth.

You want everything right now. I know, I get it. You want to be living the dream today. But, the journey is the dream. If you get to your destination in the future, what will you do when you get there? Are you going to just stop?

The time is now. In five, 10, or 20 years from now, imagine where you'll be. This is a game of long-term growth. You'll never stop leveling up, even after you have achieved your goal. This is a game of "build as you go", and every brick you lay is progress toward building something great.

Confronting adversity daily and committing to constant and never-ending-improvement is the foundation for a mindset focused on long-term growth.

Your life is a never-ending system of self-improvement. Long-term growth means you are hitting your current goals every week. Do you remember where you were a year ago? How about five years ago? Look at how far you have come. Then, visualize where you want to be five years from now. Use the progress you have made as evidence you are doing something right.

Chances are, you made progress this year, and if you didn't, that is okay, too. The journey has stops and starts, so push forward when the time calls for it.

3. Embrace your present moment and kill your fearful "what-ifs".

Catch yourself when you worry about the future. Fearful thoughts create anxiety, and you may soon find yourself asking fearful questions:

- "What if it doesn't work out?"

- "What if I fail?"

- "What if all this is for nothing?"

The "what-if" mind game can make a mess of your stride and kill your enthusiasm. When you believe in your fears more than your own confidence, you will backslide and stop scaling up.

Turn your fearful "what-ifs" into a different set of tools. Instead of asking fear-based questions that disempower you, try asking yourself these questions instead:

- What would happen if I launched my own product?

- What would happen if I married the person of my dreams?

- What would happen if I focused on saving money, instead of spending it?

- What would happen if I finished my degree and started applying for the jobs that I really want?

Our security and peace of mind are at stake when we are no longer focused on the power of the moment, but the fear of future events.

The success you are so anxious to have right now isn't just a future event, but a present-moment journey. The action you are taking right now is the pathway to the success you so desperately want.

You can only arrive there by staying centered in your present moment.

Embrace this day as an opportunity to be your best and do everything you can to make it as amazing as possible. Being patient is about loving the moment as it is happening today.

4. Remind yourself about your why.

Your journey needs a purpose. If you are working hard and just doing without having a why, the mission is meaningless.

Remind yourself why you're here. Why are you getting up every morning and doing what you do? Why are you forging alliances with people, and what impact do these relationships have on your life?

Your why is a powerful motivator. There must be a strong enough reason to take action and continue to push forward.

Create a detailed mission statement and post it on your wall, either near your workspace or your bed. Set up reminders so that you stay connected to your why.

When all feels lost, and you are filled with uncertainty, remind yourself why you persevere. What is the one thing in your life that drives you towards success no matter the odds?

Is it your family's happiness? Making an impact on the world? Greater freedom to live life by your own terms?

Your why is the internal "fuel" pushing you forward.

Build long-term thinking into your daily thoughts. Take time throughout the day to power down and check on yourself. Don't beat yourself up if you think you're making slow progress. If somebody else is running the race faster than you, let them go. You'll see them at the finish line.

Getting there first doesn't necessarily mean you won the race. You don't want to miss any steps, so take time each week to assess where you are, and the next steps you need to move up.

"Dream **lofty dreams**, and as you dream, so shall you become. Your **Vision** is the promise of what you shall one day be. Your Ideal is the **prophecy** of what you shall at last **unveil**."

— **James Allen,** author of *As a Man Thinketh*

Breaking Through Tough Obstacles

"A hero is an ordinary individual who finds the strength to persevere and endure, in spite of overwhelming obstacles."

— Christopher Reeve, the only *Superman*

According to the American Psychological Association, "Resilience is the process of adapting well in the face of adversity, trauma, tragedy, threats, or significant sources of stress", such as family and relationship problems, health issues, or a financial crisis.

A person that has mastered the art of resilience can bounce back from difficult experiences. It is the ability to forge ahead through rough times, no matter what that is.

Are you going through a difficult experience or trauma right now? Are you questioning your commitment to pushing forward? Having doubt as to whether you can get over the next hurdle? Do you think about your breaking point, and what that could be?

Relax. You are stronger than you think. You are more courageous than you give yourself credit for. Your level of resilience is always the determining factor when it comes to winning over any challenge or obstacle.

Resilience is more than just a state of mind; it is a way of life. How you approach your challenges—and the attitude you have toward obstacles—plays a huge part in how you work through difficulties. By acknowledging the trauma or difficulty and accepting it into your life, you will become better equipped to handle it without losing your mind.

If you lack the capacity to deal with life's misfortunes, you will be hit hard when they happen. You might be tempted to flee, instead of fight, or hide, instead of inviting the challenge and giving it your all.

People with strong resilience can tap into their inner strength to work through even the most difficult circumstances. How much resilience you have is dependent on several factors, but regardless, you can develop your mind to become as strong as you want it to be.

Resilience isn't something you are born with; rather, it is something you are conditioned to have. People who are well-disciplined can persevere and show tremendous willpower when it comes to facing the raw adversity in their lives.

You can condition both your mind and body to get through anything. When many would fail, you will persevere. When many would give up and fall back, you will push on and break through. When the rest of the crowd fails, you will rise and succeed.

Resilience is the absolute belief that, no matter the impossible odds or circumstances, you are destined to win. Resilience will remove the obstacles that add stress and suffering to your life. No matter what happens, you will stick with it, persevere, grind it out, and be ready and willing to stand tall when everyone else is telling you to pack it in.

If you play sports, work in a tough business, or struggle with a debilitating illness, your level of resilience determines your ability to make it through to the other side. If you win or lose it doesn't make a difference. What matters is, you gave it your all till the end.

Seven Ways to Empower Resiliency

If you've spent time working out, you know it takes time to build up strong muscles. You have to keep doing your sets and reps on a consistent basis. Apply this habit over the course of the weeks, months, and years ahead, and you will become unbeatable in the gym.

Now, apply that same mindset to building up resiliency. You need to realize that, no matter what, winning is a matter of forming a strong mindset, developed through consistent conditioning. You need to build the right frame of mind to take on everything pushing back against you.

Stop using negative excuses such as, "The world isn't fair," or "I never get a break." Nobody said it was fair, and fairness is a game for people who want it the easy way. You will always be on the receiving end of defeat if you wait on the world to favor the perfect circumstances.

Now, let's dive into the strategies you can apply to build up your resilience.

1. Remove "disaster thinking".

The greatest self-defeating force in all of us can be traced back to our thoughts. Just one negative thought can cause everything else to fall like dominoes. For example, obsessive thoughts that focus on fear of the future will create an easy path for scarcity thinking to take control of your mind.

You start thinking that no matter what, you have less, and everyone else has more. This leads to deeper fears about the future. If you have less now, won't you have less in the future, too? Of course you will. Scarcity thinking attaches itself to your brain and literally takes over. From there, all sorts of fears start to grow.

Worry and fear are like two twisters that funnel into a bigger storm. Disaster thinking always begins with a belief that the worst is yet to come. You believe all your efforts are doomed to fail anyway, so why bother?

However, you can defeat this right now by accepting this truth: Change, sickness, and death are the only constants in life that are inevitable. These events will happen. Why worry about events that ultimately happen anyway?

Now, you can see your way to becoming great. More people are defeated by their own thoughts than anything else. Thought affects everything else, too. It either turns your mindset into a powerful ally, or a fearful one. It either makes you stand up for more or knocks you down.

Resilient people think differently from the 97% of people who are controlled by confusion and chaos. When you are focused on being resilient, you know that, no matter what negativity is out there trying to break its way in, it won't topple your positive mindset.

You can crush any negative thought that enters your mind. After all, the reason it is there in the first place is because you gave it the power to grow. You give your thoughts power, and you can take it away, too.

Focus on your thinking and observe when it spirals out of control. Bring it back and train your thoughts to stay focused in the present moment.

2. Do something now.

It is easy to put off doing tasks you have a strong resistance to. We want the conditions to be right for the cause. We don't want to act until we have trained more, studied more, or built up our confidence and courage. We wait until we are fully equipped to handle the situation, but instead of acting, we waste time preparing for battle.

Yet, we never actually go to war.

It is true we have to prepare ourselves in advance for the challenges that lie ahead of us. However, look at the smaller actions you can take while you are preparing yourself for the big game.

One area that defeats us again and again is putting off until tomorrow what can be done today. The problem is, someday eventually arrives, and by that time, we realize it is too late.

Now is the only time that matters. Now is when the greatest impact can be made.

To overcome the habit of procrastination and focus on performing at peak levels throughout the day, I use a hundred-year-old strategy called "the Ivy Lee Method". It only takes a few minutes a day to set up, and it can change everything about the way you manage your personal productivity.

It works like this:

1. At the end of each workday, write down the six most important things you need to accomplish tomorrow. Do not write down more than six tasks.

2. Prioritize those six items in order of their true importance.

3. When you arrive tomorrow, concentrate only on the first task. Work until the first task is finished, before moving on to the second task.

4. Approach the rest of your list in the same fashion. At the end of the day, move any unfinished items to a new list of six tasks for the following day.

5. Repeat this process every morning.

"The world breaks everyone, and afterward, some are strong at the broken places."

— Ernest Hemingway

3. Be inspired by the greatness of others.

There are many stories of people who have faced incredible odds and survived. There are many who faced the same challenges and didn't make it through. For instance, take Viktor Frankl, who spent years in a Nazi death camp, enduring the worst way of life imaginable. How did Viktor survive, and so many others failed? Was it just luck or fate?

Perhaps both, but on a deeper level, Viktor knew to survive, he needed to see life beyond the camp, after the war. He would imagine delivering a presentation to people on what happened, and how he survived. He also thought of his wife, whom he later learned had died in another camp.

As Frankl stated: "We can't always change the circumstances thrust upon us, but we can change our attitude towards it." One of the key factors of resilience is attitude. Your attitude toward overcoming an obstacle is always the greatest tool you can focus on in any given situation.

Is there a story that inspires you to keep going when you feel like giving up? Is there someone in this world you look up to as a role model, whose message drives you to win? If there is, learn everything you can about this person. How do they do what they do? What traits make this person great?

Ask yourself: "How could my life change if I started to model this person's style? Where would I be a year from now by implementing just one of their strategies?"

Through modeling another person's belief system, habits, words, and even their body movements we can change how we think, act and feel. Take a habit that you are weak at and find someone who is succeeding where you are struggling. Find out everything you can about what they do to stay on top.

You can change anything in your life; your beliefs about money, the way you manage your health, and how you spend the first hour of every morning.

Observe the greatness of others and blaze your own trail by modeling what worked for them.

4. Abandon the obsession to change the situation.

Do you find yourself questioning the events or circumstances by asking yourself, "Why did this happen to me?" It is natural to fall into the victim role. Things were going so well, and now, you are on the opposite side of the fence, wondering, "What happened?".

Here is an example: Two years ago, a friend of mine, whom I'll call George, had it all: A wife whom he loved, and a good job. Then, one day, it all changed. Circumstances beyond his control left him without a job, and when he turned to his wife for emotional support during this difficult time, she left to find someone else who had a better-paying job and security.

From having everything to losing so much, George sank into a depression, but during this difficult time, he was also no stranger to hardships. After growing up in poverty and having to fight for most things in his life, George could tap into that strength again to pull himself through the pain he was experiencing.

He remembered something his father had said to him one day:

"If you let the people, places, and circumstances decide your fate, you'll always be defeated by other people's decisions and behavior. So, put your life in the best hands possible... your own."

George realized he could get another job, and there were more people out there he could connect with, who would be even better than the connections he had before. George focused on making a better future. Within three months, he went from zero to hero again, securing a better job and meeting someone else, who turned out to be his soulmate.

The reality is, life gives us some big challenges. What matters are not the cards you were dealt, but how you play that hand. In the moment of your life's greatest storm, you can be the solid tree that stands against the bad weather.

People who lose when life gets hard end up whining and complaining to anyone who will listen. They say things like, "Why did this happen to me?" or "Nothing ever works out, so why bother."

If you think that way, you put a mindset in motion that is destined to fail you. Catch yourself when you take the road to self-pity. Resilience begins with refusing to give in to your troubles.

Did someone dump you, and you're feeling rejected? Get out there and connect with people who love you. Did the business you've been working on for the past year go bankrupt? Take a break and set up a new business plan. Are you overweight, and do you hate looking at yourself in the mirror? Stop looking in the mirror, get off the scale, and get on a healthy diet that works.

Learn from what went wrong and try it again—without the same mistakes this time. Resilient people are fighters. They achieve greatness because they are great on the inside.

You have two choices: You can either push through your greatest challenge, or... don't. You choose to win or lose. The decision is always yours.

5. Tell yourself these three words: "It is possible."

Three of the most powerful words you can repeat to yourself right now are these: "It is possible." Resilient people, who continue to show up and play the game—even after they've failed—know the success of achieving their goal means showing up to play the game in the first place.

The odds may be against you, you may be outmatched, or people may tell you what you are trying to do just isn't possible or hasn't been done before. History is filled with the stories of people who succeeded, despite the odds stacked against them. Sometimes, they didn't achieve the objective they set out to achieve, but they hit a different mark altogether.

When you stay resilient, you maintain the mindset and belief that all things are possible. Every situation can be understood, any defeat can be turned around. When someone tells you something is impossible, remember what they mean is, it's impossible for them, but not for you.

The minute you commit to the "impossibility", you set the standard for everything else down the pipeline. You want to win at a sport? Impossible. You want to write a book? Can't do it. You want to quit your job? Not now. Believing with all your heart that whatever you want to achieve now can be done is the game-changer in making it really happen.

Look at Richard Bannister, who broke the record for running one mile in under four minutes. They said it couldn't be done, but he was resilient and trained hard for months, both physically and psychologically. He trained himself to believe it would be possible, and his goal could be achieved—even when he was surrounded by people who claimed it could not be done—and on May 6, 1954, he broke the record at 3:59.

Impossibilities can become real possibilities if we believe in them. When you believe in something so strongly that you're unwilling to accept anything else but the result you want, you are tapping into your greatest source of power. The Undefeated exist here.

6. Set a Big Goal.

For years I didn't like who I was. After believing the voices of critics, I had a hard time believing in what I could achieve. So, when it came to setting goals, I would aim low... and hit the mark every time.

Goals are positive indicators of your success. If you are working on something that could have a significant impact on your life, you will be excited, passionate, and enthusiastic to work on it. You should create goals that are larger than life, and not built on the limited beliefs of what the world tells you is possible.

Resilient people are adept at knocking down goals, whereas many others have no goals to speak of. By achieving goals many would consider to be "too difficult" or even "impossible", you are increasing your level of resilience beyond what many people will ever achieve. By doing this consistently over months and years, you will become unbreakable.

So, ask yourself this question: Is there a life goal you have been holding onto? Something you've never shared with anyone? Something that scares you so badly that thinking about it makes you sweaty with anxiety? A dream so big that people call you crazy to be even thinking about it?

You might think I'm exaggerating, but unless your goal scares you—unless it is so big that it appears impossible—then chances are, you won't be fulfilled by aiming low. You have to be willing to fail big—or else you will just fail.

7. Experience everything and welcome the fear.

Experience is a great teacher. You want to experience as much of this life as you can. Instead of holding back, charge forward. Instead of setting limits, become limitless in your approach. Instead of saying, "I'll do it later," do it now. Instead of waiting for someone else to act first, you act first.

Resilience is not a gift, but a reward. It is what you have after years of trying and failing, pushing ahead, and taking it on the chin. It is what you gain by doing all this while you are scared. Resilience is an outcome of your efforts that you can pass on to others to build up their self-efficacy.

Adapt to the ongoing changes and drop the complaining habit. Complaining holds you back and steals your ability to do something about the situation. Do you know anyone who has made a difference by complaining incessantly about a situation they can't control? It weakens you and sets you up for failure.

Be resilient by avoiding the habits that make you weak, and empower the actions that make you strong.

Break Through the Chaos

There is a saying in Buddhism: "Chaos should be regarded as good news."

You can thrive in the midst of chaos. You can find the best of yourself when bad stuff is happening, and you don't know what to do next. Chaos brings reality to an otherwise comfortable life that makes you weak.

When we avoid our problems—and the obstacles that get in the way—we might congratulate ourselves on being clever, but this doesn't mean we have won anything. We are delaying the transition of our lives, and life is about change.

By staying resilient, focused, and ready for anything, we can handle anything. You may be going through hell right now: You got fired; your marriage has ended; or you just found out that you or someone you care about is critically ill.

These are just some of the challenges that take place every day. Many are far worse, but it is not the degree of difficulty that defines you; rather, you are defined by your attitude toward any given situation, and how you handle it.

"Forget **mistakes**. Forget **failures**. Forget everything except what you are going to do **right now** and do it. Today is your **lucky** day."

— Will Durant

How to Defeat Negative Habits

*"Your net worth to the world is usually determined by what remains after
your bad habits are subtracted from your good ones."*

— Benjamin Franklin

We know that good habits play a vital role in the success of our lives.
A system of solid habits can build a productive routine and push
your personal growth to a new level. If you can develop these good
habits over the course of 60 days and set up a consistent routine that
focuses on habit development, then over the course of a few
months, you will experience a major shift in the quality of your
lifestyle.

But, what about the habits that are destroying your chances to get
ahead? What about the habit of eating junk every evening and
ending up sick more than most people? Or, the habit of spending
all your money shopping online so that at the end of the month, you
end up having to borrow from friends just to cover your bills?

Here is what **Mortimer J. Adler** said about habit-forming:

"Habits are formed by the repetition of particular acts. They are
strengthened by an increase in the number of repeated acts.
Habits are also weakened or broken, and contrary habits are
formed by the repetition of contrary acts."

While our good habits are easy to identify, our bad habits like to stay
hidden beneath the surface. Because many of these habits are so
ingrained, we rarely recognize the damage they do over months and
years of repetitive practice. Some habits are easy to see, such as
smoking or overeating. We know we do it, and we shouldn't be
doing it, but we do it anyway.

Habits don't just happen. They are formed from a young age and
transition throughout a lifetime, but if you just let your habits
"happen to you", rather than choosing the habits you need, you will
become a slave to your circumstances. You cannot be in charge of

your destiny if you are not in control of the habits that govern your actions.

Bad habits can take everything from you over the course of a lifetime, but we are not concerned with identifying every little habit you have. We just want to identify the habits that are really doing damage to your motivation and health or engaging you in distractions that interfere with your quality of life.

Charles Duhigg, author of the bestselling book, *The Power of Habit*, has said:

"Habits are powerful but delicate. They can emerge outside our consciousness or can be deliberately designed. Habits often occur without our permission but can be reshaped by fiddling with their parts. They shape our lives far more than we realize—they are so strong, in fact, that they cause our brains to cling to them at the exclusion of all else, including common sense."

A system of negative habits may be defeating you in many ways, and they are not always so obvious. If it is something you've been doing for a long time, there is no doubt you get a reward or pleasure from your habits.

Some of these habits could include:

• Watching TV in excess;

• Smoking;

• Browsing the Internet with your smartphone;

• Eating junk food;

• Worrying about things that might never happen;

• Staying up too late;

• Not drinking enough water;

• Procrastinating about doing your taxes;

- Playing video games for three hours a day;

- Impulse shopping; and

- Complaining about your family, friends, and coworkers.

Ask yourself whether you want to live the remainder of your existence doing the things you've always done, using the same worn-out habits that bring the same disappointing results. Or, would it make more sense to adopt a new way of thinking, a different way to respond to circumstances and people, instead of letting the situation dictate your next step?

Many people fail because, over the years, they have built up a pattern of self-defeating habits that beat them down, instead of bringing them the success they deserve. You know the kind of habits I am referring to. These habits steal your time, energy, and resources.

Bad habits are not easily recognized. They are like old shoes we have grown accustomed to, but there is a solution. We can create a new system of better habits. Instead of beating you down, these habits will lead you to become Undefeated. You can be the best at anything you want, if you follow a repetitive set of good actions that support your goals.

Replacing worn-out habits and removing limiting patterns are the keys to achieving long-term success. However, just stopping something isn't enough. Without replacing your bad habit with new patterns, you will set yourself up to repeat the same habits later.

For example, Dave decided to stop drinking, but he still hung around his friends and coworkers at the bar. He could have gone elsewhere, but he decided to join them when they drank and partied. Two weeks later, he was back to drinking and destroying his health.

All You Need is Repetition

Just wanting to change isn't enough. You need to take direct action toward the new behavior to remove the old one. If you fail to do this, you will risk defeating yourself repeatedly.

By building powerful, repetitive habits, you are laying down the foundation for a new life. This is your winning formula for becoming Undefeated. For example, if you want to lose weight, you have to be willing to stop eating as much and focus on consuming the right foods.

Just saying, "I am done with sweets," isn't good enough. The moment you feel weak—which is usually later in the day, when your willpower is at its lowest point—you'll resort to eating a big snack for the sugar rush, just to start feeling normal again.

Those who relapse in recovery—even after years of abstinence— venture back to what's most familiar, even though it almost destroyed them. Even after years of staying on course, if we are not diligent about sticking to our newly-formed habits, the bad habits that caused us grief will return—and in greater force this time.

So, if you are tired of bad habits robbing you of the better life you can have right now, I have a simple system to help you replace unwanted behaviors with healthier choices.

Build Better Habits: The 10-Step Approach

1. Identify the specific problem the bad habit is causing you.

For this system, I'll use Ted as an example. Ted, like many people, uses his phone 3-5 hours a day. He uses it most in the evening after work. Ted has identified this as a bad habit because he has stopped reading books, which is something he used to do a lot. As a result, his mind isn't as sharp as it used to be and using his phone into the late hours is affecting his sleep.

2. Identify the habit you want to stop.

Ted wants to stop using his phone at night—specifically, after 7 PM—and he will use that time to read instead.

Now, identify the good habit that will replace the bad habit.

Replace phone time with reading time. Ted will read from 7–9 PM, and then do some light exercise.

3. Create an action plan for the next 30 days.

The goal is to commit to a set action plan for each day. This can be as simple as committing to five minutes per day doing a single action.

For example, if you're trying to build the exercise habit, you can do just five reps on the first day. If you are writing a book, commit to writing for 10 minutes a day for the next 30 days.

What matters isn't how much we get done. The idea is to follow through with the action and make it a consistent pattern you will perform every day, regardless of whether it is 10 reps or 50. You can scale up later, when you are conditioned to perform the action without thinking about it.

4. Review your progress after 30 days.

How consistently did you follow through with the action? Did you miss any days?

How would you measure your success, compared to 30 days ago? You can review your progress by asking yourself: "How do I feel now, compared to 30 days ago?" This is easy to map out. If you have been sticking with your course for 30 days, the progress is obvious.

5. Reset the clock for another 30 days.

Continue to take consistent action for the next 30 days. Determine how you can make improvements. If you missed a certain number of days, try to miss even less next time.

At the end of 60 days, how has this habit transformed the way you live? Did you lose weight, get stronger, or feel better because you meditated for 60 days, instead of surfing the 'net and playing with your phone?

6. Set realistic expectations.

Change takes time. We have to be patient with our progress and resilient in our approach. The people who become masters at what they do reach that level through decades of practice.

If you have had the same habit for years, it is deeply ingrained into your mind. Expecting to replace your habit with a new one takes time, and it could take up to six months. Even then, you have to continue practicing the new habit.

7. Be aware of your triggers.

Just as we need triggers to take direct action toward building positive habits, we also need to be aware of the triggers that pull us back into bad habits.

For example, when I reduced the amount of junk food I was eating, I had a habit of strolling through the junk food aisle in the store. As soon as I walked into the store, it was the first section I visited. Then, if they were having a sale on chocolate that day, my trigger would associate cheap chocolate with pleasure, and I would give in.

Whatever habit you're working on replacing, make yourself aware of the habits that trigger you to give in and eat, spend, or indulge. The danger lies in our own minds. It is your thinking that causes you to seek out the trigger spot. You might be working on replacing smoking with exercise, and then, after a workout, you stroll by a cigar shop because it's on your way home.

In the early stages of habit-changing, we are vulnerable to our cravings, and what a mentor of mine called "crooked thinking." Make yourself aware of the habits that draw you into relapsing.

8. Focus on long-term conversion.

It takes time to change behaviors. If it happened quickly, everyone would be doing it. According to a study released in the European Study of Social Psychology, a team of researchers led by Phillippa Lally surveyed 96 people over 12 weeks to find out how long it took them to develop a new habit.

At the end of the survey, Lally analyzed the results of the experiment and determined the time it took to form a new habit was approximately 66 days.

We need to think long-term. It takes approximately 66 days to replace a habit. This is a tough road to navigate for most people.

We need long-term focus and consistent concentration over a period of months to make it happen. If you are expecting to see massive gains after two weeks, you could be setting yourself up to fail. Think long-term habit change and stay focused on daily repetitions.

An example is running. If you are not used to running, but you want to join a marathon in six months, you will have to spend months building up endurance to achieve that distance. Start by running a kilometer a day the first week. The next week, take it to two kilometers.

In the third week, scale up again. Eventually, you'll be conditioned enough to run the full course. If you miss a day, pick it up the next day. If you miss a week, adjust accordingly, because you will have lost initial momentum.

You can use this system for anything: Writing a book; lifting weights; or meditating. Start small. Scale up gradually.

Meanwhile, the bad habit that was stopping you from acting in the first place will lose its power if you stop exercising it. So, instead of eating snacks every night, work out and get into shape. Instead of watching TV, write 500 words a day and get your book done.

You get the idea. You will build a system of undefeatable habits by following this protocol.

9. Build support through accountability.

New habits are difficult to implement and stick with—especially in the beginning. For this reason, having a habit buddy is a recommended approach to supporting your new routine.

If you're trying to get into the habit of exercising more, this could be someone you go jogging with twice a week, or you might do strength training together. If you can't meet in person, you can connect via Zoom, Skype, or Google Hangouts.

Set up a habit accountability call with your friend once a week to follow up on progress. Make sure you work with someone who is also interested in habit development—although they could be working on a different habit. It's important to share not just the fun of habit-building, but the struggles you are going through, as well.

10. Throw out the all-or-nothing approach.

If you've had a slip, get back into it. We all miss a day in our routine. What matters is you can pick it up again the next day. If you let it go too long, you risk starting over again. If that happens—and it probably will—begin again. The only time you fail is if you give up and revert to your old habit.

Let yourself make mistakes along the way and learn what works and what doesn't. Changing a habit is about consistency. It's not about how much or how many, but how often. This is the frequency with which you act.

If we expect perfection, we can also expect failure. An all-or-nothing mindset often stops people from setting up new behaviors. I don't know anyone who has a perfect track record. Habits take time and persistence, but most of all, patience. We have to be ready to forgive ourselves again and again. I have broken several bad habits this way, but in some cases, it took years.

Your bad habits only have power over you because you haven't truly taken positive action that is consistent and accountable. If you follow the system that I laid out here, you can use this to break any habit and start a new one.

Imagine what could happen a year from now, if you eliminated three of your most destructive habits and replaced them with energy-driving, efficient habits.

You would become one of the elite **Undefeated** performers.

"Because some people see a wall and assume that's the **end** of their **journey**. Others see it and decide it's just the **beginning**."

— Angeline Trevena

The *Achilles Heel* of Self-Defeat
(and How to Prevent Getting Caught Off Guard)

"Don't be caught off-guard. Be ready for when that day comes, and you know that life is going to get the best of you."

— A. P. J. Abdul Kalam

There is an enemy we all have living inside our own minds. This enemy is so secretive that you barely know it exists. That enemy is your own mind, and if left to control your thoughts, it will consistently feed you lies.

Your internal lies feed you loads of fake stories about who you are, and what you are capable of, and your lies convince you that you are who you are, and nothing you do will ever change that.

The Weak Link and Achilles Heel

In Greek mythology, Achilles was a Greek hero of the Trojan War. According to legend, Achilles—who was a powerful warrior and believed to be undefeatable—was killed after being shot in the heel by an arrow. Not even Achilles could have predicted this was how he was going to die.

Achilles died because he failed to recognize his weak spot.

So, this brings us to the question: "What is your Achilles Heel?"

We know we have areas in our lives in which we are not particularly strong, and while it may not kill us—as it did Achilles—we could end up setting ourselves up for defeat, if we fail to see what is holding us back.

We do lots of things to keep ourselves strong. You might eat all the right foods, exercise regularly to develop physical strength, or practice the philosophy of sages to keep your mind sharp. It is one thing to be defeated by someone else, but it is quite another to be defeated by your own ignorance, arrogance, ego, or naiveté.

Then again, sometimes we lose in life because we just can't see deeply enough into our own world. It takes others to show us what we need to work on to be better, faster, stronger, and more in sync with ourselves so that we can stay a cut above the rest.

The fact is you may never know where you are weakest until it is exposed by a failure, and by then, it may be too late. You will go down for the count.

Tyson vs. Douglas: A Case Study in Self-Defeat

Prior to February 11, 1990, Mike Tyson was the undefeated heavyweight champion of the world, with a string of titles that included the WBC, WBA, and IBF, all of which he held simultaneously. This placed him as the world's undisputed heavyweight champion, and pound for pound, Tyson was ranked the best fighter in the world.

Buster Douglas, on the other hand, was the underdog, regarded as a good fighter but never great. He had never trained properly for other fights and lacked the luster to really push his abilities, but that changed with this fight.

Buster's mother had died just prior to the fight, and he had greater motivation than ever before to make this fight count. He trained harder than he had for previous fights, whereas Tyson had trained the least.

Tyson had several areas of weakness that set him up to lose the fight against Buster Douglas. Aside from poor management and coaching, Tyson wasn't mentally prepared to fight Buster Douglas. His Achilles heel could be blamed on several key factors: Partying, women, drugs, more women, and poor training habits.

No matter how you analyze it, bottom line is, his head wasn't in the game. He lacked focus.

He didn't think he had to train because he was "undefeated"; he had never lost a fight.

When it came to showtime, anyone could see the difference in each fighter's style. Douglas was unafraid and advanced on Tyson continuously throughout the fight, despite getting knocked down in the eighth round and recovering (albeit with a slightly longer count advantage). Tyson, on the other hand, didn't throw much, and due to Buster's longer reach advantage, was kept off-balance throughout most of the fight.

In what could have been predicted as an easy win for Tyson because of his history as the undefeated champion, it turned into one of the biggest upsets in boxing history. In the 10th round, a determined Buster Douglas unleashed a series of blows against Tyson—including an uppercut, followed by four hits to the head—that put Tyson on the canvas. He was KO'd, and Buster Douglas became the new heavyweight champion of the world.

Despite the controversy surrounding the fight, there are certain facts that contributed to Mike Tyson's first loss of his life: A lack of training, lack of focus on winning, and Tyson didn't have that "edge" that had brought him so far. While Mike Tyson wasn't anticipating a loss, he had set up his defeat long before the fight.

Closing Weak Links

Failing to close the weak links in our systems is what sets us up for failure in the future. If you have an event coming up that you didn't train for, you risk not delivering the best presentation. If you know something needs to be done and you procrastinate instead, you run the risk of losing out on an opportunity.

It is these weak links that throw us off-balance. Not setting ourselves up for success weeks before our biggest challenge is at hand can result in getting "knocked down to the mat."

Just as Tyson (and much of the rest of the world) underestimated Buster Douglas, it suggests that there are going to be days when you will never see defeat coming.

While you are busy focusing on the left side, something is coming at you from the right.

So, how can we protect our "fortress of solitude" from getting destroyed, when we have to focus on so many things without getting blindsided by an unseen enemy?

You have a weak link that is setting you up for failure. You don't know what it is yet, but it is there. There is nothing to be ashamed of, because we all have this. It sets us up for the fall and hits us when we least expect it. This could be a lack of awareness, a bad habit, an addiction not yet dealt with, or an old self-defeating belief.

Knowing what your Achilles heel is and identifying it before you fail can make all the difference between falling hard or not at all.

For example, one of my weak points is poor planning. When it comes to setting goals, working on a financial plan, or preparing for the future, I just go with the flow, let life happen, and ignore the planning that could have saved me pain, if only I had learned this essential skill.

Eventually I realized that, by ignoring the plan, I was setting up my own knockout. What I learned from years of failing forward is, you always need to be ready. You never know when that "right hook" is going to come out of nowhere and land home.

I am a procrastinator by habit. Developed from a young age, I ignore the tasks I find uncomfortable, boring, or I have resistance toward. Over the years, this has cost me money and employment opportunity. This Achilles heel defeated me by setting up failure in every way possible. When I had enough, I decided to get serious and do something. Until I recognized this as a damaging and destructive force in my life, I hadn't done anything about it.

I started keeping a procrastinator's list, based on an idea by author Rita Emmett, who wrote a great little book called The Procrastinator's Handbook. By taking intentional action every time that I had the urge to put off a task I knew had to be done, I was able to heal the wound that had plagued me for most of my life. By seeing the problem for what it was worth, I was able to move myself from being defeated and helpless to being Undefeated.

As Winston Churchill said, "By failing to plan, you are planning to fail." Do you want to fail or succeed? You know you want to charge forward and win.

Do I still have the urge to procrastinate? Yes—but the difference is now, I see this as the chink in my armor that was destroying everything. By choosing not to see it, I was losing every time.

This is why it is vital you recognize the chink in your armor and patch it up. What is your Achilles heel? What is the one thing you do consistently that could crush your chances of success? What are you avoiding that you should pay attention to?

Do you procrastinate? Do you not pay attention when people are speaking to you? Do you watch too much TV or engage in activities that consume your time? Is there a lack of attention to your financial situation? Are you putting your health at risk by eating too much or consuming the wrong foods?

Here are the Top 10 "Achilles Heels" people struggle to overcome. See if yours is on the list:

1. Overconfidence

2. Lack of Knowledge

3. Procrastination

4. Poor Health

5. Underestimating Your Opponent

6. Scattered Focus

7. Lack of Attention

8. Negative Mindset

9. Limited Thought Patterns

10. Narcissism

Your Achilles heel takes many forms: habit, behavior, mindset, mental and physical forms, or all of the above. We are not perfect, but we need to recognize this imperfection and strive for continuous improvement. If we don't, then when we're least expecting it, we'll be knocked down with a right hook we never saw coming.

Now, if we had been trained to know that right hook was coming— in other words, by studying our opponent's strengths—we could have been ready for it when it happened.

> "I have learned that champions aren't just born; champions can be made when they embrace and commit to life-changing, positive habits."
>
> — Lewis Howes

It doesn't matter if we are in sports, arts, business, or parenting, we all have areas in our lives that need to be improved. You have many weaknesses—as we all do—but we don't have to fix everything. Just focus on course-correcting the one "Achilles heel" that has the greatest impact on your future success.

Is your Achilles heel a habit that has been defeating you for many years? Is it someone in your life who is treating you badly, but you won't leave the relationship? Is it your own level of thinking that prevents you from moving ahead?

Figure out what this is and craft a plan to remove it from your life. Something is always holding you back. This is nothing to be ashamed of. It is life. There is no such thing as a smooth ride—even when you think you are doing things well. Oftentimes, it takes a good friend or someone close to you to point out what your Achilles heel is.

So, now that we are aware of the Achilles heel that could be setting us up for failure, what is your "weak link"?

You won't always see defeat coming, but you can prevent it the best you can by taking these measures. To eliminate the weak links that increase the risk of self-defeat, here is a four-step action plan:

1. Create an action plan and schedule time for these actions leading up to your goal.

2. Eliminate the unnecessary.

3. Identify previous setbacks, and the reason you failed.

4. Train for 30 minutes a day.

Action Plan for Beating Your Achilles Heel

Step 1: Look back and make a note of the last three setbacks you have had. Do these setbacks have something in common?

Step 2: Now, what is the one area of your life in which you fail on a consistent basis? Is it your health? Chaotic relationships? The area of your life bringing you the most grief is telling you that there is a problem here.

Step 3: Make a list of the solutions you could start to work with. In the case of my procrastination, I made a list of tasks I had been putting off. I had things on my list dating back years. I was paying for it with guilt. Now, what can you do? What is the one small action you can take that scares you but needs to be done?

Step 4: Make this daily action a habit. Create a trigger, so you recognize when it is acting up.

Step 5: Be sure to recognize the positive changes in your life by doing something about this. The chink in your armor that has made your life a living hell is now no longer a burden. You might have multiple chinks in your armor, but this is one less.

Step 6: Continue to focus on developing a system of continuous self-improvement. Don't let yourself fail.

Don't be caught off-guard. Be ready for when that day comes, and you know life may get the best of you. Fight back and get up when you get knocked down.

You will always have a weak link in your routine, habits, or way of thinking. Make a list of what these weak links are and continue to hack away at eliminating them.

There is a way to stop defeating yourself. First, admit there is a problem, look at the negative impact it is having on your life now and in the future, and then, devise an action plan to rid yourself of it.

The weak spot is a point of **vulnerability**. It leaves you open to defeat, but the greatest defeat you face is the defeat of yourself by yourself. You can become a person who is Undefeated by acting on the things that close that gap.

"**Life** is truly known only to those who suffer, lose, endure **adversity**, and stumble from defeat to **defeat**."

— Anais Nin

Fuel Your Enthusiasm and Do the Work You Love

"There is a real magic in enthusiasm. It spells the difference between mediocrity and accomplishment."

— Norman Vincent Peale

Enthusiasm is the fuel that keeps your internal energy charged up. When winning seems hopeless, and defeat is imminent, an enthusiastic mindset, followed by a course of action, will defeat any fear or uncertainty that stands between you and everything you have ever wanted. To stay in the game of winning, you have to play the game until the end.

Pay attention to the inner passion that screams, "You're not done yet!"

Many people who don't finish what they start end up failing because they lose enthusiasm, or they failed to build it from the beginning. Your success is highly probable when you tap into the power of an enthusiastic mindset. On the other hand, your failure is decided when you lose that enthusiasm.

How do you build enthusiasm in your life? Where do you discover this dynamic energy source that has the power to drive achievement beyond all boundaries?

You keep going when you tap into your enthusiasm. It is raw energy. It is fuel for success and can drive you to keep working when most people have thrown in the towel. To be Undefeated, you must have enthusiasm and be able to call on this wave of energy when needed.

Enthusiasm is contagious. You can pump others up when their drive and motivation is weak. Your enthusiasm can get others to rise and respond with action, instead of buying into passive observation. Enthusiasm is the foundation of passion we hear so much about from people who have been there and made the best of a bad situation.

Why the World Needs More Enthusiasm

Too many people are defeated by a lack of enthusiasm in their lives. You can see these people numbering in the thousands, as they move on the street, clutching briefcases, brows furrowed in serious faces carved from stone, trapped in the years of doing work they never wanted to do to begin with.

So many are locked into a life that feels hopeless without any hope of getting better, living a life of desperation and wishing they had made better decisions. They continue feeding into this pattern for many years to come.

One course of action that will always influence your direction is the attention you pay to your life choices. If you want more passion in your life, you have to act like a passionate person. You need to generate it from within and stop looking to the world to deliver it. The mind of an enthusiast works this way.

When you feel a genuine love for who you are, you are naturally enthusiastic about living life in such a way that people are drawn to your energy.

Have you ever been around someone who was so genuine, positive, and passionate that they made you feel enthusiastic, too? If so, then what I have been saying all along is true: Enthusiasm breeds enthusiasm. You can change not only your own state, but the state of anyone else around you, if they are willing to be open and accept this gift.

People who are not passionate about who they are or what they do struggle to find enthusiasm for anything. They move through the days like zombies, seeking out cheap forms of entertainment, looking to be distracted, so they don't have to face the truth: Life is empty because they are not happy. Life is chaotic because they feed into this chaos. These people are not defeated by the world; they are defeated by their own way of thinking, their own beliefs, and their limitations set by thought patterns they are too stubborn to break.

Think about something that makes you genuinely happy. This sounds like a very simplistic approach, but how complicated do you want to make it? It isn't complex or beyond your scope of possibility. How happy are you when you are being the person you love the most?

Stage performers have said they were never more alive than when giving their best in front of a crowd. Public speakers would come to life when switched on to speak to a crowd of fans. What action or ideal makes your heart stir with excitement?

Find that, and you will discover the answer to everything you have ever wanted. Better yet, when you share this passion with another human being, they become immersed in your enthusiasm and want to contribute more to the world.

I have seen people dissolve all their fears by awakening to the greatest mystery in the universe. They have the soul of a searcher who never gave up on the journey.

Are you ready for that step?

I believe you are.

Do you know what defeats the average person? It isn't a lack of resources, or a lack of ideas. It isn't about being the most intelligent person in the room, or the best athlete on the field. It isn't about who you know, or how much you know or don't know. It is about knowing what you truly want at the deepest level, and knowing you are born to do great things with the life you have. Your thoughts and actions should be in alignment with the vision of this greatness.

The path to greatness and building an undefeated mindset begins with your first step: the tennis player who picks up a racket for the first time, the author who starts writing their book with the first sentence, and the actor who stays up late, rehearsing lines and getting into character. Your greatest wins are driven by the desire to rise above your biggest challenges, and in most cases, that is fear.

Your enthusiasm is the driving force that pushes you to keep leveling up, developing into a stronger and more confident action-taker. It is the spark that ignites your imagination. It is the single idea that transforms your life. When an idea grabs hold of your mind, the next course of action is to find a way to turn this idea into a reality.

Your imagination, and the vision it creates, will become the foundation for winning big on your chosen path. What most people call *fantasy*, you call the *future*. What many say is impossible, you say is possible. What defeats the average person is your leverage to becoming undefeated.

> "Enthusiasm is the yeast that makes your hopes shine to the stars. Enthusiasm is the sparkle in your eyes, the swing in your gait. The grip of your hand, the irresistible surge of will and energy to execute your ideas."
>
> — Henry Ford

Enthusiasm for Work You Love

According to Gallup polls, 85% of workers surveyed anonymously worldwide admitted to hating their jobs. This is a shocking number of people who wake up every day to spend 8–12 hours doing something they don't like. You might be reading this now and realize you are one of those people.

So, how can we have enthusiasm for the work we don't want to do?

The artist loves their work because they are creating. A parent builds a life at home for the family. Teachers bring enthusiasm into the classroom, and the students are inspired by this.

Enthusiasm is not just a feeling of euphoria. It is an action driven by charged emotion. When you are doing something that makes you feel alive, enthusiasm is the natural feeling that results from performing the work you love. This could be working with people you want to help, or a project that is going to have a long-term impact on the future of your business or others people's lives.

The people who do work worthy of a day's efforts will always give their best and go that extra mile when they are feeling excited for what they are doing. Drudgery and laziness stem from doing the kind of work you are just paid for. We have all been there; we have all had jobs we didn't like, but we had to put in the time for a paycheck. We show up and put in the time, but the job becomes a rut. Enthusiasm cannot thrive in this environment.

Discover what you love to do and push all your free time into making it successful. Is there a business idea you have? A sport you want to pursue? A new career opportunity, pulling you to quit your boring work and do something else more deserving of your time?

Enthusiasm Defeats Negative Behavior, Fear, Doubt, Procrastination, and Excuses

Self-defeating behaviors, such as negative thoughts, procrastination, and self-pity, will be crushed by the force of your enthusiasm, but, how do you learn to control it? How can you direct your enthusiasm to act in accordance with your purpose and plan?

As a recap of earlier points, here are 4 tips you can use:

1. Be intentional about spending time with passionate, enthusiastic people. I know that this seems like common sense. Unless we are a negative person who enjoys the company of misery, the friends and people we spend time with have a direct influence on our enthusiasm.

Find these people and make them a part of your life. Fix your energy so that it helps feed them and keep them close to you. Release the people around you who destroy this enthusiasm. You're not doing them or yourself any favors by holding on anymore.

Tony Robbins said that Proximity is Power! You need to be surrounded by the energy of enthusiasm in order to harvest this into creative action.

2. Bring your joy forward. With pen in hand, I want you to write down the one thing that makes you feel alive. Is it an act that you perform, such as giving to people? Or, a line of work that fills you with such energy that you'd die if you couldn't do it for the rest of your life?

Whatever this is, make it your primary goal to turn it into a full-time job. Let this work define you, instead of allowing other people to decide what does. A life of joy and fulfillment can only be lived when you do what you love to do with people you enjoy being with.

3. Develop your action plan. What will you do each day to bring you closer to your primary goal or objective? Review the discussion on setting goals. Set aside 30 minutes at the end of each week to write your goals for the following week.

At the end of each day, take a few minutes to write three priority tasks for the next day. Do it the night before, instead of waiting until morning. You can also break these goals down into monthly and yearly goals.

Always be prepared and have a plan for what you are working on. Get fired up about your life! Make a move toward the things you once thought were just a dream. Instead of flying without navigation, your plan is to be your own navigator so you can achieve everything you've ever imagined.

4. Pass it on to others. What is the point of living an Undefeated lifestyle, if you don't share it with others? Teach them the way to improved happiness and greater fulfillment. Pass your message on to the people in your life. Love these people by sharing your best and hold nothing back. Be as enthusiastic for the success of another as you are for your own success.

There will be many times when you will lose your enthusiasm for work, play, and even love. You will start to question your direction, purpose, and intent.

When your enthusiasm starts to drop away, here are 14 steps you can implement to ensure you stay on top of your game, and keep your positive energy flowing.

14 Steps for Building Energetic Enthusiasm

1. Start each day with 10 minutes of quiet reflection time.

2. Ask yourself, "What is my main focus point today?"

3. Review your life plan, and the milestones towards building that plan.

4. Connect with a mastermind group of positive thinkers and action-takers.

5. Spread your enthusiasm to others. Help them discover the best within themselves.

6. When defeated by competition, or someone else's decisions, don't let it deter you. Failing your way to success is the path of many.

7. Create a mission statement and review this once in the morning and again in the evening.

8. Do what you love to do. When you can't always do that, make it your chief objective to turn your deepest passion into a full-time job.

9. Write down five things you have deep gratitude for every day.

10. Pray for someone who is going through a hard time.

11. Brainstorm the solution to your most demanding obstacle right now.

12. Identify the one area of your life in which you're procrastinating. Then, write down three action steps you can take to overcome this area of procrastination.

13. Commit to living a fearless lifestyle. Make this commitment every morning, before you start your day.

14. Stay healthy. You will always gain the most from your enthusiasm if your health is in top form. Eat right, train and exercise, and avoid habits that suck your energy away.

"If you have **passion**, there is no need for excuses because your **enthusiasm** will trump any **negative reasoning** you might come up with. Enthusiasm makes **excuses** a nonissue."

— Wayne Dyer

Visualizing the Big Win

"Visualize this thing you want. See it, feel it, believe in it. Make your mental blueprint and begin."

— **Robert Collier**

Athletes have been using the power of visualization for decades to win at the sports they try so hard to master, but how does this work? Do we just imagine what we want and expect everything to show up? Is this some kind of "believe in the universe, rah-rah" strategy?

Here is why visualizing your big wins in life turns you into a winner: First, we need to think about visualization as both a technique and a mental habit that works the same way as weightlifting. When you show up every day at the gym, and you work your muscles, they grow, and you get stronger. If you do this on a consistent basis, you make considerable gains over a shorter period.

Now, imagine if you used this same concept and spent 20–30 minutes a day visualizing yourself succeeding at what you love. This goes against much of what we are used to doing. The fear of failure can be so strong that many people are trapped in its cycle without realizing it. How often do you visualize yourself not making it? Do the images running through your mind support or destroy you?

See yourself succeeding at your current goals, and your visual imagery will build the steps required to take you there—but the opposite can be true, too. If you visualize yourself failing in life, this fills your thoughts with worry and anxiety.

Your resulting actions will be built on this visual model. Your subconscious only listens to the commands it is given, and so, what you imagine as true becomes your reality, based on the visual imagery running through your brain.

See yourself succeeding at what you love, and you will build the bridge from here to there. This is what we refer to as the "Mental Rehearsal" technique.

The Mental Rehearsal Technique

With external imagery, athletes will visualize themselves competing, as if watching it happen from a spectator's viewpoint. By implementing this visual imagery, using both internal and external visualization, world-class athletes can achieve their dreams and improve their performance.

This works because—like working out with weights—you're now exercising your mental pathways and rehearsing the steps you need to take to make it. Building this vision is the first step to creating a framework for everything you have ever wanted to achieve.

By training your mind to see what success looks like, it starts to put the pieces into place. You notice the actions you need to take, and then self-doubt and uncertainty slip away. You erase the pathways that once focused on constant failure.

Instead of shooting in the dark and hoping to hit your target, you are going to see your target in clear sight, know what it is and how to get there, and then, take the steps needed to cross the finish line.

> "One needs something to believe in, something for which one can have wholehearted enthusiasm. One needs to feel that one's life has meaning, that one is needed in this world."
>
> — Hannah Senesh

Tapping into visualization methods and focusing on your goals has several key benefits. It programs your brain to attract what it expects and desires. It builds up your motivation to work harder for your dream, and in doing all this, it calls upon the law of attraction to draw toward you the resources, opportunities, and people needed to make it all happen.

A Mental Rehearsal Exercise

Now, here are the steps to putting the mental rehearsal technique into action. You only need a few minutes a day, but it can add significant value to your quality of life.

Find a place to relax and get comfortable. Imagine yourself performing a set action/task directly related to your master goal. If you want to be a writer, see yourself writing and typing for hours on the keyboard, nonstop, with the ideas just pouring out of you. Then, visualize yourself holding your completed novel at a book signing.

For a business owner, what does your company look like in five years, as you expand your clientele, reaching thousands of potential new customers? If you are a homemaker and raising a family, how do you visualize the growth and success of your family, as they learn from your wisdom and teaching? If you are a public speaker, what would it look like to pack thousands of people into your event?

As you visualize this, I want you to tap into your feelings. How do you feel, knowing you are doing something that has meaning and fills you with greater ambition, while expanding your passion?

Tapping into your emotions is a big piece to the formula. You can change your current state of mind and emotions by creating the same state you want to experience in the future. You see, when people say that they want to be happy, it is because they are waiting for something to come along and give them that happiness, but they don't have to wait for anyone or anything to change their emotional state.

They can do it right now, in this moment, by imagining what their lives will look like when they are at complete peace. What action steps would it take to get you there? What would you need to do starting today to change the way you view the world?

A part of the formula for being Undefeated is recognizing the emotions that will make it so. The super-achievers—those who make dreams come true—aspire to become Undefeated by learning to master these emotions. Being happy requires making a decision, and then following up with the right action. Your energy, motivation, drive, ambition, and passion derive from this place, where you imagine what can be, and then do whatever it takes to get there.

Tapping into Your Visual Power

If you model the people who succeed at their goals, there is nothing lucky about their success. Chances are, they use some form of visual meditation to see the place where they want to arrive. There is a delicate balance here, too.

While you are projecting your thoughts into the future and seeing who you want to become after getting there, you must remain in the present moment, so you can concentrate on pushing forward with consistent action. If you spend all your time dreaming about the future but doing nothing about it in the present, you will fail to make any progress, and the result will be defeat.

So, how do we tap into this **visual power?**

Chances are, you do it every day with your thoughts. You create images and situations in your mind. We have 50,000 thoughts a day, but unfortunately, most of our imagination is used to create situations based on worry and fear, and self-defeating scenarios.

Most people set up their path to failure long before they arrive there. You see it every day. You've seen it in yourself, I am sure. You failed a test because you visualized getting an F—even after studying. You didn't get a job because you were running a constant vision through your mind of seizing up in the interview—and so, you did.

You can name dozens of situations in which you failed, and if you could go back and analyze your thoughts in that moment, you'd find your visual imagery had something to do with it. In fact, it may have had everything to do with it.

> "Successful people maintain a positive focus in life, no matter what is going on around them. They stay focused on their past successes, rather than their past failures, and on the next action steps they need to take to get them closer to the fulfillment of their goals, rather than all the other distractions that life presents to them."
>
> — Jack Canfield

Visualization keeps you focused as you develop a clear line of concentration. Your imagination is always seeing, planning, and putting together the pieces of your dreams to create what you want. When you focus on a specific goal, you are directing all your mental energy toward an objective that becomes the vision of what you want.

By visualizing your success, you are creating a framework to build upon. A life is measured by the amount of visual planning that supersedes it, not necessarily by the amount of work put into achieving a goal.

We can win in seemingly impossible situations. Like the athlete who refuses to give up because of a handicap or disadvantage, you can use what I refer to as "intentional visualization" to master your actions now and build a direct path to the big win.

Remember, your adversary is not your biggest challenge. You are your biggest challenge. Most people defeat themselves before anyone else has a chance to.

How do we defeat ourselves? By visualizing our failure, instead of our success. Have you ever dreaded a test the day before and feared getting a low score? If you did, was your score as low as you expected? Now, think about this as a situation for success.

Now, you can try this strategy to visualize your victory before you arrive. I call it "optimum visualization", and it is a powerful form of mental training that harnesses focus and brings your thoughts in alignment with what lies ahead of you.

Optimal Visualization

I want you to think about something you want to achieve. This can be a skill you are trying to improve, or a goal that has been in the works for many years. Choose this one thing and make it your one big goal. Block everything else out.

Now, what is the first action you will take to begin working toward this goal? See yourself taking this one action right now.

Concentrate and focus on this goal for 10–15 minutes. Think about nothing, except for this one thing. By focusing on this and thinking of only what you want to create, you are directing all your present mental forces into this visual creation and feeding your imagination with a stream of positive energy. This is a form of **laser-focused**

concentration that has massive potential to **turn a dream into reality** when directed with intentional purpose.

Now, believe this goal is becoming your new reality. If self-doubt or uncertainty creeps in, just acknowledge it is there. This is okay. You don't have to resist your negative thoughts. When you hear your internal voice say, "Is this possible?", you can respond with, "Hell, yes!"

Then, visualize yourself as living in your new reality. Are you living in another country, helping people? Do you visualize yourself telling your boss, "I quit," because you are becoming an entrepreneur? Are you training for a sport or practicing a musical instrument? Can you see yourself doing this? How does it feel?

Our visualization invokes powerful emotion. This emotion is real. It fills you with positive influence because you begin to believe it is already happening. You can make it happen.

Try optimum visualization for at least 10 minutes a day. If you have the time, a 30-minute session is recommended at least three times a week. Keep in mind this is a form of meditation that requires your absolute commitment of concentrated mind energy. If you just do it whenever you feel like it or occasionally, the results will be minimal.

Commit to this challenge for 30 days. Start off slow, in 10-minute increments, and build up gradually, until you are eventually performing this for 30 minutes. Once you can sit through a full session and concentrate fully on succeeding in one area of your life, you will have built a solid foundation for personal excellence.

Daily Visualization Training: Your Action Plan

Simply visualizing isn't enough. You need to take your deepest passions and put them into action by building solid intentions around everything you want to create. To do this, you can:

- Use visual meditation for 20 minutes each morning. Visualize the reality you want to experience.

- Create a master goal for your life. Spend 20–30 minutes each day imagining the success of this goal. See yourself succeeding at this goal.

- Play inspirational music to keep you inspired and motivated. As you listen to the music, visualize the activities you will perform to take you closer to fulfilling your vision.

- Practice the optimum visualization technique to accomplish amazing results! Plan at least three sessions a week.

- Start a visionary journal or blog and record your thoughts and visions on paper. This enhances your experience of the creative visualization process.

"**Visualize** this thing that you want. See it; feel it; **believe in it.** Make your **mental blueprint** and begin to **build.**"

— Robert Collier

Rising Up and Rebounding After the Knockdown

"I've missed more than 9,000 shots in my career. I've lost almost 300 games. 26 times, I've been trusted to take the game-winning shot and missed. I've failed over and over and over again in my life, and that is why I succeed."

— Michael Jordan

It is in our moments of failure when we discover who we really are, and what drives us to achieve the impossible against insurmountable odds. In other words, when the odds are stacked against you, it is your decision that changes everything.

When facing defeat, will you let yourself be kicked down? Or will you tap into your inner drive to rise and take back what is yours?

One of the core keys to overcoming adversity is killing your excuses. There are several people who seemingly suffered a great defeat or were placed in a situation in which they had to get up and make the most of what they had.

Life isn't always fair, but how many times have we said, "Life isn't fair"? Well, since when is it supposed to be? Look around at the world. Every day, people are suffering, have no food, lose loved ones, and go through serious, life-changing experiences.

Life isn't supposed to be fair at all. It is our expectations that set us up for a quick defeat. If you think you're entitled to a good life, you may want to reconsider.

Entitlement leads to defeat in all kinds of cases. You might be handed a serious blow, but hitting the mat isn't the problem. It is whether you stay down and accept it is over.

Can you accept your defeat—and, if you can, are you willing to accept the outcome of giving up and deciding you've had enough?

Nancy Kerrigan vs. Tonya Harding

Nancy Kerrigan and Tonya Harding were both competing in the Olympics back in the early '90s. Up until this point, they had been going hard against each other in competition, with Harding landing a triple axis in the 1991 US Figure Skating Championships, winning first place, and Nancy Kerrigan getting the bronze medal.

During the 1992 Olympics, Kerrigan won the bronze medal, and Harding took home fourth place. The pressure was on, and both women were gunning for the top spot.

In January 1994, Kerrigan and Harding were practicing for the US Women's Championships in Detroit. The results of the competition would determine who would enter the Winter Olympic Games in Norway.

The night before the qualifying skate, as Kerrigan was walking off the ice, she was attacked by an unknown assailant who had been hired by Tonya Harding's ex-husband (a fact revealed later in the investigation).

The attack left Kerrigan injured, but not entirely crippled. The qualifying skate was the next day, and Kerrigan—despite leg pain—decided to enter the competition anyway. Kerrigan showed up to win, just hours after the attack, Undefeated, on the ice. She took the silver medal. Harding, on the other hand, came in eighth place—in part, because of a broken lace.

She later denied any knowledge of the attack when questioned, but her career as a skater was permanently damaged.

Character Wins Every Time

Defeat comes in many forms. There are times when many people try to cheat their way to the top—but even if they win, they lose. We never get ahead in life at the expense of another person's loss or by inflicting damage on their lives.

Character is built by deciding to win when the odds are not in your favor. By becoming an Undefeated superstar, and by pushing against the odds when they are pushing back, you are creating an unbreakable mindset. In the end, it is character that matters most, not winning, fame, or fortune. Character.

If you clamber to the top, and you get there by injuring, defaming, or causing mental or physical harm to others, you lose. You might get the "trophy", but the real prize—the elevation of your character—will be forfeit.

Instilling integrity is always your greatest victory.

Pushing Back Against Loss and Defeat

Steve Jobs and Apple

In 1985, Steve Jobs was fired from Apple, the company he had created. Jobs spent time thinking about what he wanted to do with his life, but during his absence from Apple, Jobs created the company neXT, which Apple later bought. When Jobs returned, he brought his innovative ideas for the iPhone and iPod that would take the company to a whole new level.

Walt Disney

Walt Disney was fired from his job as an animator for the Kansas City Star newspaper. The reason was his editor thought he lacked imagination and creativity, and he had no good ideas.

After going through bankruptcy because he had acquired a studio called Laugh-O-Gram, Walt Disney and his brother, Roy, set up the Disney Brothers Studio, where they created the classic animated films that went on to garner 22 Academy Awards.

J.K. Rowling and A Boy Wizard

J.K. Rowling is quoted as saying, "You might never fail on the scale I did, but some failure in life is inevitable. It is impossible to live without failing at something, unless you live so cautiously that you might as well not have lived at all—in which case, you fail by default."

J.K. Rowling's dream was to be a writer. In fact, she was so passionate about it that she would spend time at her day job crafting stories about Harry Potter. She got fired for that and lived on her severance check, while she pounded out her stories that would go on to become worldwide bestsellers, but her story of defeat would continue for several years.

After a brief marriage ended, Rowling was jobless and living on social security as a single mother. Nearly to the point of being homeless, she spent her days in cafés, creating the Harry Potter series. Through the years, J.K. Rowling forged on through depression, doubting whether she would make it as an author, but even with a finished manuscript, the books were rejected by a dozen publishers—until they were accepted by Christopher Little, a small publisher in the UK.

Abraham Lincoln and the Weight of Loss

Abraham Lincoln suffered immeasurable loss and defeat in his life before he became the 16th President of the United States in 1861.

His family was forced out of their home in 1812, and he had to work to support them. His sister died in 1831, and he lost two business ventures in 1831 and 1833, respectively, which sent him into bankruptcy. Engaged to be married in 1835, his fiancée died, and in 1836, he suffered a nervous breakdown.

Between 1832 and 1860, leading up to becoming elected, he ran in eight different elections and lost all of them. He had four boys with his wife, Mary Todd, and three of them died before maturity.

In 1860, Abraham Lincoln was elected the 16th President of the United States. Lincoln would go on to preserve the union during the US Civil War and bring about the abolition of slavery.

Remaining undefeated until the end—when he was assassinated in 1865—Abraham Lincoln serves as an outstanding model of both resilience and determined grit.

Robert Downey, Jr., Addiction, and the Great Comeback

Although he had a steady stream of success in the 1980s, Hollywood-blockbuster star Robert Downey, Jr. nearly lost everything to drugs and alcohol. For years, he struggled heavily with drug abuse that ultimately landed him in prison.

After being in and out of jail—and being found in one incident wandering around barefoot—Downey was fired from his current work in TV and theater. Officially broke, the actor was sent to rehab again in a last-ditch attempt to clean up.

In many ways, his situation was deemed hopeless, and he wasn't expected to live much longer if he continued this course of self-destruction, but after responding to an ultimatum posed by his wife, Downey decided to get serious about getting clean. He picked up a lead role in The Singing Detective and went on to bigger projects that included The Avengers and Iron Man.

Robert Downey, Jr. turned what looked like an impossible situation around and refused to be defeated by his addictions. Now, he is one of the highest-paid stars in the movie business.

Rising After the Knockdown

These stories have a common theme: People who refused to give up and pushed forward, despite the odds stacked against them. In the face of death, addiction, bankruptcy, or mental breakdowns, there is nothing that can defeat you—except acceptance.

You can accept your fate and let it take you. You might go through a failure or difficult time, such as losing your job or struggling with substance abuse, but what matters isn't the weight of the challenge in front of you. We all go through something in our lives. It is inevitable.

What makes the difference is what you decide to do about it. Will you say, "I've had enough," walk away, and do something else? Maybe, and if you do, that is okay. This decision could take you in another direction, but if you really believe what you are fighting for is worth it, you have to push through—no matter what.

You have to stay Undefeated in your resolve to see this through to the other side. You have to weigh the risks of what might happen if you keep failing, and the risks of what you stand to lose if you do nothing and quit.

To rebound from a loss or setback, we have to let go of the losses and focus on the gains. Yes, you may have lost the race, but you can get back in the game and become stronger than ever. Failing is the path to victory and losing tests your resilience by challenging you to rise to the problem, instead of shrinking back.

Undefeated champions are not just tough on the outside. On the inside, they value survival against incredible odds. This is the journey toward real growth. If you want to develop on a personal level, it is about acknowledging the challenges that stand between you and everything you have ever dreamed of having. If something is in the way of that, you must find the solution to remove it.

In the stories above, our Undefeated champions could have given up at any time. Abraham Lincoln could have quit after losing his first election—or even his seventh!

Steve Jobs had enough money to live like a king—even after getting fired from Apple—but he wasn't a quitter.

After being rejected by multiple publishers, J.K. Rowling could have decided maybe they were right; boy wizards weren't going to be popular.

We can make it through rejection, knockouts, job loss, bankruptcy, or even death. We can make it through the worst of our storms. You are stronger than you might be giving yourself credit for. When adversity kicks you in the face, it isn't the end of the fight. It can be just the beginning. As endless success stories have told us time and again, people are as strong or as weak as they set out to be.

When defeat is pushing you down, and all the odds are stacked against you, what will you do? When everything hangs in the balance, how will you respond?

Rebound Action Strategies

Here are three Undefeated strategies you can put into play when the odds are stacked against you, and it looks like failure is the only option. Remember, failure is the way to victory.

1. Pick up, be crazy, and start something else.

Back in the 1980s, Mark Cuban, lost his job as a computer salesman after defying management and making a $15K sale on the side. After he got fired, Mark went to work and formed the company Micro-Solutions. He has made billions from that company, and since getting fired years ago, he has never looked back.

When you get knocked down, look for the next best thing. You don't have to go back to the way things were. Mark could have easily tried to find another job as a computer salesman. Then, what? He would have sold some cool stuff for another company.

Losing his job was the best thing that could have happened. It showed him he was meant to climb higher and do something more than sell someone else's crap.

The lesson here is when you are tired of working for someone else, start your own thing. Do you have an idea or a business plan to build something? Build it before someone else does. Do people tell you you're crazy? Tell them they are right; you were because you knew inside yourself there was something you should be doing, and you were not acting on it. That was crazy.

2. Stay resilient... no matter what.

At the age of 74, Colonel Sanders had over 600 franchises featuring his famed fried chicken recipe, but before that, the colonel had been fired from several jobs because of his temper tantrums and went bankrupt at the age of 65 after closing his restaurant. Then, Colonel Sanders traveled the country, living in his car and trying to sell his chicken recipe.

Despite the setbacks and the string of failures that seemed to follow the colonel wherever he went, his efforts and ongoing resilience paid off. Today, there are over 18,875 Kentucky Fried Chicken restaurants in 118 countries worldwide.

3. Build your passion into a thriving business.

Before Thomas Edison became a world-renowned inventor, he worked at Western Union—that is, before he got fired for conducting experiments in his office.

However, that didn't stop Edison. He was born to build, and he went ahead with his inventions full-time, eventually launching his first patent two years later. Throughout his lifetime, Edison accumulated 2,332 patents for his inventions and eventually created Edison General Electric (later to merge with Thomas-Houston General Electric) to form General Electric.

Thomas Edison's inventions and passion to create launched patents and inventions that changed the world. His passion for creating and inventing what many people thought impossible proved he lived a daring and Undefeated life. Failure after failure, he succeeded.

"**Falling down** is not defeat. Defeat is when you **refuse** to get up."

— Paulo Coelho

Maximize Your Energy and Increase Vitality

"The higher your energy level, the more efficient your body. The more efficient your body, the better you feel, and the more you will use your talent to produce outstanding results."

— **Anthony Robbins,**
Bestselling author of Awaken the Giant Within

Mentally preparing yourself to deal with any situation is critical to developing your ability to handle defeat. In addition to training your mind to handle tough obstacles, you have to be physically fit, as well. A body that is functioning at its best will be less fatigued and tired. You'll be better equipped to be Undefeated if your physical condition is primed with energy.

You can give yourself a significant advantage if you work to level up your energy. This will increase your enthusiasm, build greater positivity, and fuel your ambition to take on any challenge.

When we are feeling weak or physically ill, this can affect our drive and enthusiasm. It is tough to stay on top when you are out of shape, eating poorly, and not taking care of your physical health. Your health—physical and mental—is everything. Let yourself go, and you will increase the risk of becoming defeated in situations where you could easily be winning.

Fatigue—both mental and physical—can fail you when you need strength coupled with perseverance the most. So, don't be caught off-guard by letting yourself go.

I believe maintaining a high level of energy is one of the core ingredients to sustaining the momentum that will allow you to continue pushing forward. Exhaustion can cause you to slow down and feel defeated, and then, eventually, you may be reduced to crawling instead of walking, and then, doing nothing at all.

Take care of your physical and mental health, and you will be able to sprint for a long time, instead of just running hard for a short distance.

These tips on raising your energy are not new concepts, but I'll give you a formula you can turn into a habit, which will raise your energy and keep you Undefeated. By setting yourself up with a system that keeps your energy level high, you will have more natural strength. You will have better sleep, and you'll need less of it.

To boost your energy levels, there are five areas I'll focus on:

1. Rest and Sleep

2. Food and Diet

3. Exercise

4. Water

5. Breathing

You might be thinking that to boost your energy and get the most out of your energy, you need to join a gym and spend thousands of dollars on "super" vitamins that promise to extend your life if you take them three times a day. Everything you need to boost your energy level is available to you right now. Most of the stuff you need to promote good health and stay that way won't cost you a thing.

Most of the energy we expend and lose is lost on stress, overworking ourselves, and participating in activities that steal our strength, instead of building it. Your physical and mental strength have everything to do with how successful you are. If you feel sick, sluggish, or fatigued, this affects everything else, and you'll be less likely to want to fight back or push forward.

Here are the essentials to boost your vitality and stay Undefeated in times of stress or when facing adversity. I realize many of these are already common sense, and you may already know this information, but knowing and doing are two different things.

I want to give you a plan of action to build your vitality, day by day. There is a very simple action, step, or process for each of these areas that does not require you to give up large amounts of time or stick with a lengthy diet program.

The bottom line: You can increase your energy and build vitality without changing your lifestyle drastically. If you want to be Undefeated, you have to start by building undefeatable habits that focus on strength, instead of weakness.

Let's say your Achilles heel is an addiction to sugar, smoking, or poor exercise habits that drive you to fail. By using what is already available to you—water, air, and space—you can make significant changes in your quality of life. We need water for hydration, air for breathing and cleaning our blood, and a small space for working out (that does not necessarily mean the gym).

The Importance of Water and Staying Hydrated

You should drink an average of 8-12 glasses of water a day. Your body is made up of 75% water. So, it makes sense to eat foods made largely of water and balance this with water intake. So, how can you be dehydrated when surrounded by fresh water at home and in local supermarkets?

We often go for the easy fix when we are hungry, such as sugar-based foods that steal our energy and increase our weight in the form of body fat. Who needs that?

So, the common-sense approach is to stay hydrated. This will improve brain function and keep energy levels stable. You can get dehydrated during the day without knowing it, and then, a sluggish, fatigued condition will hit you in the middle of the day.

Recommended Action Tip: Drink a 750 ml bottle of water when you wake up. Keep a bottle with you throughout the day. Drink more during/after a workout.

Food Choices and Energy

You want to boost energy and vitality? Start with your food habits. My habit for years was to consume large amounts of sugary foods, such as snacks, chocolate, and gummy bears. I'd gorge on this stuff daily—in addition to eating—and it didn't matter what time of day it was. I suffered from fatigue and exhaustion all day long.

When a doctor asked me about my daily intake of foods, his advice was so simple, I could have saved myself the trip: Stay off the sugar. So, I started cutting back gradually and left carbs out of the picture—especially after 4 PM. Breaking the habit of not snacking was tough, but I knew it was a necessary course of action to improve my health and restore my energy and vitality.

Vitality can change your life because it changes the way you feel. A sluggish lifestyle, in which you feel like crap most of the time, is directly related to eating poorly, bad sleep patterns, a lack of exercise, and a lack of water (dehydration) or fluid intake.

Sleep: The Critical Element

Many people have irregular sleep patterns. We either get too much sleep or not enough. Three reasons for feeling exhausted and going through your day fatigued with a lack of energy are:

1. Lack of sleep

2. Poor food choices

3. Stress and worry

Here is a list of suggestions to help you build better habits and improve your quality of sleep.

Wind Down an Hour Before Bedtime

For many people—including students in high school and university—their screen time is running over eight hours a day. Between computers, smartphones, and iPads, we are online more than ever. For many, this means right up until bedtime, and often, in bed, we have our phones right next to us so that we don't miss those late-night emails and notifications. In fact, the #1 disturbance for sleep is now linked to having a phone within reach while sleeping.

The solution: Put it on the other side of the room and set to quiet mode. Turn the vibration mode off. Go a step further—turn your phone off until morning and power it down at least an hour before bedtime. Do this, and you're going to get great sleep, wake up less during the night, and have more time for reading or other offline activities in that critical hour before bedtime.

You should aim for six to eight of sleep per night. This varies, but you know your body better than anyone, and how much sleep is acceptable for you.

The other habit you can implement is to stop snacking or eating heavy foods several hours before sleep. This hits two areas that increase energy. First, by not eating several hours before bedtime, you let your body prepare for sleep when it needs the energy to mend and rest.

Eat before bedtime, and this throws everything into chaos. I know people who eat potato chips, chocolate, popcorn, or heavy meals right up until they go to sleep. How do they feel most days? Sluggish, tired and complaining of weight gain.

Preparing for a good sleep:

1. Power down your devices an hour before bedtime. To help with this, set up a reminder—such as an alarm—to go off. When it does, you are done with any devices.

2. Put a cap on snacks and eating three hours before sleep. If you must "munch," eat fruit such as a banana, or drink vegetable juice. This is easily digested, unlike heavier food that sits in your stomach while you are sleeping.

3. No more caffeine after 6 PM. I would say earlier than that, but I know many people love coffee after dinner. You could switch to green tea, a probiotic drink, or Kombucha tea, but anything caffeine-based is going to play havoc with sleep patterns. If you are in the habit of drinking coffee late at night, set up a reminder several hours before bedtime and use it as a cut-off time.

4. Eliminate heavy carbs and overeating at night. Rice, pasta, and bread are heavy in carbs and steal energy from your body because they require a lot to digest. I would suggest replacing your carbs later in the day with something like tofu or fish. Lean meat, walnuts, apple slices, or raw vegetables will only add to your increased vitality.

It's a scientific fact that so much of your energy comes from having solid, quality sleep. The habits you practice every day—from food choices to the time you start preparing for sleep—can change everything. Take note of what you are doing at night that could be sabotaging your sleep and setting up your defeat for the next day.

Begin now to adopt new habits to move you to a pro-active pattern of behavior and away from undesirable habits.

> "The only way to keep your health is to eat what you don't want, drink what you don't like, and do what you'd rather not."
>
> — Mark Twain

The 20-Minute Workout

Unless you are training for a triathlon or, trying to gain enough muscle to compete in the next Mr. Universe contest, you can get away with working out for just 20 minutes a day. Not everybody has two hours a day to block out to visit the gym, get changed, hit the floor, and do an intensive 60-90-minute workout.

While exercise may feel like one of those things you should be doing because you're out of shape, or you gain weight every time you eat ice cream, it can be done in just 20 minutes at home with little equipment.

I recommend the 20-minute medicine-ball workout. You can get one on Amazon for less than $40 and if you learn to use this correctly, you won't need anything else—especially not an overpriced gym membership you can't afford and can't make time for. Don't just exercise when you feel like, it or are guilted into it when you notice you've gained another pound. Start small and build up to longer sessions.

You can also include other easy-to-do activities, such as push-ups, stretching, and skipping. A jump rope is less than $10!

You don't need me to tell you exercise builds energy into your day in more ways than watching TV or surfing the Internet does.

Here is a brief breakdown of what your exercise routine could look like:

1. Stretch for 5-10 minutes before your workout.

2. With a medicine ball, try a set of six exercises for 10-15 minutes. You can find a list of exercises and routines here:

3. At the end of your workout, you can celebrate with a protein shake, or a glass of fresh vegetable juice.

Deep Breathing Practice for Reduced Stress and Increased Relaxation

One of the most natural forms of activities for living things is breathing. Although we don't always think about it because it is automatic, our breathing plays a large role in our mind and body's energy.

Deep breathing is a form of exercise. By doing so, you are giving the body what it wants the most—oxygen! Engaging in 3-5 sessions of deep breathing every day improves blood circulation and increases your body's vitality and energy.

Breathing properly begins with an awareness of your breathing patterns. By breathing full, complete breaths, you can significantly improve your overall health. Your breathing patterns are influenced by many factors—particularly, your emotional state.

When you feel stressed, angry, fearful, or anxious, your breathing is affected. For example, when you are under immense stress, you might hold your breath without realizing it, or when you are anxious, you may reduce your breathing to short, rapid bursts.

Throughout the day, our breathing patterns may vary from slow and controlled while sitting at a desk, working, to rapid breathing or short bursts when we are under duress, pressure, or prolonged worry and stress. This defeats our vitality.

Slow, relaxed breathing helps reduce stress and worry and clears your mind of worrisome thoughts. It reduces blood pressure and calms your heartrate. I think of deep breathing as a form of meditation without the lotus position. All you need is 5-10 minutes of focused time.

Here is how you can focus on deep breathing:

1. Situate yourself in a comfortable position. You can sit up straight or lie down.

2. Breathe in through your nose and focus on your lungs as they fill with air.

3. Hold your breath for three seconds and exhale.

4. When you breathe in, visualize drawing positive energy into your body. On the exhale, imagine the negative energy leaving your body.

5. Do this for five minutes. Over time, build up to 10 minutes of focused breathing.

Work Less, Relax More

This is the last piece of the formula, and it is one that many ignore. Overworking—meaning, putting in over 60 hours a week—is stealing time away from all the other activities—not to mention reduced family time. So, if you work your ass off all week, you won't have much energy left for anything else.

You'll work out less—if at all—be prone to fatigue from less sleep, and dehydration may go unnoticed. With the additional stress and focus on the job, your breathing may be shorter than usual.

We all work to pay the bills—regardless of whether you go to a company each day, or you work from home—and many people are asked to work more than they should.

So, for any of this to work, your focus on how much you are working should be a requirement. If you are too busy to implement any of the steps mentioned here, nothing will improve. You will go on feeling fatigued, stressed, and exhausted.

Here is a brief setup for you to consider working less:

1. Discuss the possibility of **reduced working hours** with your boss. Imagine what you could do with 10 hours of extra time per week, or 40 per month? I did this last year and was able to reorganize my schedule, so I was out of the office 90 minutes earlier. I made less money for the year, but the added benefits of having more time were well worth it.

2. **Reduce your screen time** both at work and at home. When you are looking at a screen, are you working, scrolling, or just clicking through crap? Many are, and this is hard on both the eyes and the brain functions. Turn off your devices or walk away from them for an hour a day.

   Schedule an hour when you will not look at any screens. Then, the following week, increase that to 90 minutes. Like most people, you rely on technology to do your work, but spending 6-8 hours in front of a screen is hard work.

3. **Discuss the possibility of flex-time**. You could work from home one day a week or set your own hours at work. If the company values you as an employee, they may be open to negotiations to assure you are happy in your position.

4. **Keep your to-do list of action tasks** to under six for the day. Use the Ivy Lee Method to get your critical tasks done.

Setting Up Your Energy-Boosting Action Plan

Now that you have read through this material, you have a grasp of habits that create a body and mind with increased energy.

Here is what I suggest starting with: You can integrate the habits of exercise, vitamin intake, and sleep to develop a system in which your energy levels get a significant boost and stay there.

1. Begin to reduce your sugar intake. When you get the craving for something sweet, before deciding to eat a sugar-based snack, replace it with a piece of fruit.

2. Plan for sleep. Avoid eating heavy meals several hours before bedtime. If you must eat late, cut your portion in half and fill up on vegetable juice or a shake.

3. Commit to a 20-minute exercise program four times a week. You can extend this to 30 or 40 minutes, depending on your time frame. Use the medicine ball technique, jump rope, or stay-at-home activities that require little equipment or cost. You can always visit the gym, if that is your preference, and you have the time.

4. Implement the deep-breathing strategy into your routine twice a day. Follow the steps and reap the benefits.

5. Work smarter, not harder. Restructure your work day and working culture.

"Success is almost totally dependent upon **drive** and **persistence**. The extra energy required to make another **effort** or try another approach is the **secret of winning**."

— Denis Waitley

The Habit of Deliberate Practice

"I've always found that anything worth achieving will always have obstacles in the way, and you've got to have that drive and determination to overcome those obstacles en route to whatever it is that you want to accomplish."

— **Chuck Norris**

Motivation will take you halfway, and determination will push you the rest of the way. This is the place where the habit of deliberate practice is born, but what does it mean to practice your actions with deliberate intention?

We are making decisions all the time. Most of these decisions are habitual and so ingrained that they don't seem like decisions at all. For example, if you are in the habit of eating a bowl of cereal every night before bed, you are responding to a routine and habit that has been ingrained into your psyche. You might even have that snack at the same time and prepare it in the same manner. You aren't even thinking about it after a while.

But, what if you decided having this every night before bed isn't healthy and, to lose weight and feel great means you have to deliberately stop yourself from responding to this craving when the urge to eat hits you?

You are now making a decision that goes against the ingrained habit. You are breaking the chain of a habit that was holding you prisoner. Break the chains of this entrapment and free your mind of this obsession, whatever it might be.

People who go to the gym regularly, read regularly, or learn from online courses regularly are following the practice of deliberate action. You are choosing to do something because you got a good result from it, and now, you want more of it. Deliberately deciding to act and practice a habit until it becomes a part of you is what deliberate practice is all about.

Building a Foundation for Deliberate Practice

We know change takes effort, perseverance, resilience, and inner strength. When you change yourself, you build on your commitment to practicing a habit or activity with deliberate intention as the pillar of becoming an **Undefeated champion.**

It is the deliberate practice of an athlete who wakes up at 5 AM and puts in the practice for the big game that wins the championship. It is the deliberate practice of the prolific public speaker who shows up on an empty stage and rehearses their lines that moves thousands of people at a live event. It is the deliberate practice of the entrepreneur who rises at 5 AM and begins the day of strategic planning for the empire they are building from scratch.

It is the consistent habit of deliberate practice that is the difference. It makes everything move forward from a place of passive activity to an action-driven game plan.

The question is are you ready to do whatever it takes to become Undefeated in your personal and business life? Are you ready to act with direct intention and take deliberate action when called upon?

I believe you are ready, or else you would have given up by now. Even if you think you aren't there yet, imagine you can be, with a clear sense of focus and clarity on your objectives.

Deliberate practice refers to a special type of practice that is purposeful and systematic. While regular practice might include mindless repetitions, deliberate practice requires focused attention and is conducted with the specific goal of improving performance.

In Tokyo, the most revered sushi chef, Jiro Ono, is a master of his trade. Jiro is the owner of Sukiyabashi Jiro, a three-Michelin-starred, internationally-renowned Japanese sushi restaurant in Tokyo. For over 70 years, he has been mastering the art of making sushi. When you work for Sukiyabashi Jiro, you spend your working career performing the same task repeatedly, day in and day out, doing the exact same thing you did the day before.

This system marks the discipline of excellence. By performing the same action continuously for months without end, you build an unbreakable habit. You maximize your performance in the long run by breaking down each individual stage, one step at a time.

Focus and the Power of Intention

Focus is the key. You must be focused on the task at hand to master the basic principles. If you try to be everywhere, doing everything and scrambling to stay on top of the latest trends and the latest tech gadgets, or stay one step ahead of the competition by bouncing from idea to idea without implementation, you will not master anything but chaotic disruption.

Chaos results from haphazard habits. The people you learned about in this book developed the habits of Undefeated champions. Determination will only take you so far, but a commitment to the practice of this one skill drills focus into laser-precision action. It is the difference between a shotgun approach and a one-shot rifle.

The greatest obstacle people face is lack of focus on one course of action. Instead of mastering a skill—such as learning the three most common guitar riffs or writing 1,000 words a day—we jump all over the place.

Scattered focus means weak results and wasted energy. When we fail to nail our goals, we feel like failures, but failing isn't the result of doing the wrong thing; rather, it is the result of doing the right thing the wrong way.

This is the power of intention, knowing why you are doing it as you narrow in on the vision for the life that is being created by you. Regardless of the distractions pulling at your attention, you have the power of decision to control the direction of your actions. What you invest your time in becomes the yardstick that measures your success or failure.

Deliberate practice can only be mastered when you are prepared to take deliberate action. What will you focus on for the next five minutes? The next day? The rest of the week?

Focus is the action taken when you know the direction you should be moving in. You need absolute clarity on what your mission is. If you don't have this clarity yet, what is your intuition telling you?

Focus comes with developing this clarity, and a sense of purpose. You don't have to pretend to know the outcome of the journey, but your direction must be clear. Focus is the compass that will lead you towards completing key objectives and merging with the right people to get things done.

There are many brilliant people through the centuries whose stories serve as strong models for what is possible. By tapping into the reservoir of the higher consciousness guiding you forward, you will stop the guesswork. You will no longer drift along, waiting for luck to make you successful.

Every destination starts out with nothing more than an idea or synchronistic intuition to do something, but eventually, it leads the entrepreneur, artist, or leader to the end of a road that has been there the entire time.

Focus and deliberate practice go hand-in-hand. You can only be deliberate when you concentrate on the actions necessary to take another step forward.

Implementing the Deliberate Practice Model: You don't have to wait for that perfect day before you start to act with deliberate practice. You can begin by building awareness into your actions. I have never known anyone to accidentally achieve a lifelong goal or succeed by just blind luck. Without intention, you end up living in the land of confusion.

Deliberate Practice and Scaling Up High Performance

If you were to ask a high-level performance expert the secret to success, I doubt they would say it was due to luck. Nothing is by accident. We may get lucky breaks along the way, but performance is always the result of deliberate practice, showing up at the time you planned for and doing what you intended to get things done. The deliberate performance model breaks the mold of procrastination and delivers measurable results.

The Drive Behind Deliberate Practice

Break the mold. Do something you "can't" do. In most of our daily work or hobbies, we are engaged in familiar activities. As creatures of habit, we repeat many of the same tasks but never improve on them. Your deliberate focus needs to be concentrated on not just doing the task or work but doing it differently and better than you did it the day before.

This is what we mean by "scaling up". We do what is comfortable, so we don't exert ourselves or burn ourselves out, but we have to push beyond what we know and into the unknown. Only then does it start to make sense.

The foundation of becoming a person who is Undefeated is training your mind, body, and spirit for war. You are not at war with the world, but instead, you are at war with yourself. Your old training is holding you back. Deliberate practice is designed to push your boundaries, not confine you with them, and we are rarely challenged to push beyond what we know—or, worse yet, what we think we know.

The world will not defeat you in the end... you will defeat yourself. If you can recognize this and train yourself to see the areas you can improve for greater endurance, better productivity, or leveling up your writing or creativity, then you are ready to play in the big leagues.

Take any pro who is the best at what they do—or, even the second- or third-best. Ask these people, "What is your secret to success?", and they will tell you, "I did what everyone else was doing. I just did it more consistently, and I did it a little differently every time."

So, what do we know about deliberate practice? It has very little to do with genius or raw talent and more to do with conditioning your mind and body to perform at a level of excellence. If you observe the performance of superior athletes, musicians, or entrepreneurs with an insane level of productivity, you will see a group of similar traits they have in common.

Most high-performance athletes or prolific artists were exposed to the craft they mastered at some point in their lives. There is such a thing as an innate ability or "gift", but, for most people, it is a result of repetitive action, driven by a well-crafted purpose, plan, and accountability. Here are the six elements of building deliberate practice and being purposeful in your intentions.

Critical Steps to Develop Deliberate Practice

Work on Improving Your Skills by 1%.

The only standard for improvement is to be committed to a level of constant and never-ending improvement. Any individual or organization that is not directing itself or its people to become better each day soon finds itself eventually closing shop. You always need to do things slightly different than you did the first time to make gradual but incremental improvements.

By committing to the 1% improvement plan, you can make small changes daily, instead of big changes that have little long-term impact. Every business that continues to grow year by year is working on improving its products, systems, and people. These are known as tiny gains, and, if performed diligently, they can have a big impact on your performance over the next year. So, how can you improve by 1% and continue to build better performance in your life and work?

1. Declutter your desktop by deleting one file a day.

2. With every workout, push yourself slightly more than you did the day before. Do an extra pushup or one more rep.

3. Wake up just one minute earlier, until you are getting up at 5 AM.

4. Are you writing a book? Write an additional 20 words each day. Work your way up to doing 2,000 words a day, if that is your goal.

5. Reach out to one new sales contact every day. If you get rejected, keep reaching out. Count your rejections as they come pouring in.

The best advice a mentor of mine once gave me was, "Most people are doing what they have been trained to do—what they are told to do—but they only act when someone is paying them to do it." We don't give it 110% if our deliberate practice is for someone else. Self-motivation is an inside job. It comes from knowing you are working for something that is bigger than yourself.

Regardless of who you are, how much you train, or even the support you have backing you, there will come a time when you don't feel like training, going the extra mile, or even working up enough energy to step outside the house. Everyone has a breaking point, a point of resistance that tells them, "I've had enough for today," or "Can't we take a break from this?"

It is normal to feel this way. You might start beating yourself up and thinking you're lazy, but if that were true, you would not have made it this far, and you wouldn't be reading a book on how to become an Undefeated champion. In fact, pushing yourself too hard could do more damage, instead of having the opposite effect of toughening you up.

You could compare yourself to masters of the trade and see how they show up each day to put in the work "at the gym" or their "fingers on the keyboard", but one of the keys to deliberate practice is in knowing when to practice, and, in most cases, scheduling this practice into your day. You need to be clear on your deliberate actions and where they are going.

Here are the strategies to implement right now. Focus on one strategy, until it has been absorbed by your mind, and nothing can break it.

Schedule one hour a day to do your training.

What are you committed to becoming better at? How much time would you need to commit to this to make it work? No matter what it is, you need to schedule your time, so you can practice. If you don't schedule it, chances are, it won't get done. Do you want to work out and train more? Schedule 30 minutes in the morning. Do you need to work on your new business? Schedule one hour in the evening, just before dinner.

Focus on your One Thing for the duration of this hour.

Scheduling your actions is one thing but staying fixed and focused is another. There were many times when I scheduled writing time to work on a novel; only 10 minutes later, I was off doing something else. When you set up your time to work on your one thing, start with 30-minute increments and work your way up to one hour. When you have mastered this time block, increase the amount of time you can commit to deliberate practice.

Visualize your actions working towards your goal.

Visualization is used by architects to imagine the final design of the building they are working on. It is used by professional athletes, authors, artists, and businesspeople. Why is visualization so important? How can you know what you want if you can't see your success beyond tomorrow morning?

When you are clear on what matters most, visual interpretation aligns your actions with your vision. It is like laying out your map before taking the journey. Before you go anyplace, wouldn't you feel better if you knew beforehand how to get there?

Identify disruptors that interrupt your training flow.

Distractions are abundant. We are challenged by our instant access to everything these days. It is critical to choose how to invest your energy and power. With so many energy thieves fighting for your time, you have to draw boundaries and know when to say no.

Say no.

These two words combined will bring you more peace of mind and free up your space to focus on the greater skills that will move you to empowerment. What distractions do you fall prey to? How do you set up your daily routine for success or failure?

Take frequent breaks.

Deliberate practice and staying focused means giving your mind and body enough time to rest. The one-hour focused model works if you can maintain focus that long, but when you find yourself getting fatigued, stop and break. This could include walking away from your work for 20 minutes or taking a 30-minute nap in the early afternoon. I take a nap in the afternoon, and three 15-minute breaks throughout the day.

By resting throughout the day, you give your top-level functions a break, and a chance to heal. This improves your ability to practice your skills and push forward with a renewed enthusiasm.

Build an identity through your actions.

Keep something in mind. Everything you learned up to this point won't make any difference if you don't take care of your physical and mental health. This means exercising, getting enough sleep, eating well, and drinking enough water. For your mental health, meditation and reading are two activities I would recommend.

You need a body that is functioning well to avoid fatigue, and a mind that is performing at its best for improved concentration. If you get sick, it is too difficult to maintain any kind of quality focus. When you are ill, that becomes your focal point. Make healthy living your priority, and then, it will have a positive impact on your intentional actions.

Create a mental representation of your objective.

What would it look like if you became a person who could run a full marathon? Write the book you have been talking about? Deliver a lecture in front of a thousand people, despite your fear of public speaking? The mental vision you construct for your objective is a roadmap. It shows you the logical steps needed to go from here to there. We know we have to take action to get better, but what are those actions, and how are they structured?

Get off the plateau. Years ago, I used to spend a lot of time in the gym. I worked out for years and made incredible gains by transforming the way I looked, but one day, it just stopped, and I got bored when I worked out. I no longer looked forward to the workouts. So, I took up karate for a year. The same thing happened. Boredom set in after 18 months. When I looked at the possible reasons, I could recognize the pattern I had been following most of my life that prevented me from achieving excellence. I would trap myself by burning out, growing bored, and not changing the method I was using.

When I hit a plateau, I tried to get over it by working harder, but I was still doing the same exercises. Hiring a personal trainer and coach, he was able to show me how to get unstuck. We need to be deliberate in the approach to excellence. Like steering a ship, you have to course-correct every now and then. Otherwise, you will end up somewhere else, drifting. Boredom is a sign that you need to change something, but you can deliberately change your routine at any time.

Don't wait until you hit a plateau before switching your habits. Plan and do something different, before you become bored. By that time, you will start to skip the gym or stop writing for a week to take a break, but that opens the floodgates of procrastination.

"You're the average of the five people you spend most of your time with."

— Jim Rohn

Coaching, Accountability, and Deep Encouragement

It is tough to make it on your own. We all need that "coach in the corner" or "cheerleading squad" to push us to the end of that line when the going gets tough. Therefore, I suggest hiring a coach, or, at the very least, finding an accountability partner. If you are playing a sport, you should join a team or a club, so you will be surrounded by people with like-minded interest. Are you writing a book? Join a writers' group online or in your local area.

The area of your life that is getting your attention needs support, encouragement, and a way to measure the progress you make.

Having said that, you do have to put the work in. Nobody can force you to reach out for help. Surround yourself with the people who will push you forward. It is the crowd you hang with who will become your biggest fans. They are there to help you celebrate big wins. They will also help you with losses—and eventually, everyone loses at least once.

However, losing is important—just as important as winning. You have to lose to win. Knowing one without the other tips the scales. You need to recognize and be made aware of your own mistakes. Then, once you have identified what they are, course-correct every time it happens. This can work with any habit or behavior.

We all need a coach in our corner, the one person who is ready to point out our mistakes and encourage better ways to do something that save time and energy and improve the ability to concentrate.

Hire Your Mentor: I discovered earlier in life that to overcome most obstacles, you need help. This is where the power of a mentor comes in. If you don't have a mentor, I strongly suggest you find someone. A mentor and an accountability partner are different. Your mentor can look at things objectively and guide you towards a viable solution.

Whether you are attempting to improve in sports, art, music, or even make a better home for your family, trying to succeed by yourself by reading books, watching YouTube, or taking online courses can only take you so far. However, working with someone is groundbreaking. A coach or mentor can point out the subtleties of your performance and correct critical errors you may miss.

For example, David Allen, the productivity guru and bestselling author of Getting Things Done, charges $20K an hour to enter someone's life and work with that person all day to improve systems and get rid of inessentials, and by approaching the situation objectively, he can see the areas where his clients are failing.

What does this have to do with intentional action? Everything. You could take intentional action and do the wrong things or do the right things in the wrong way.

Find someone to help you scale up, whether that be a coach, a friend you are working with to hit your goals, or your spouse. You will increase your success rate by partnering with the right people.

As Good as It Gets

If you have ever seen the Jack Nicholson film, As Good As It Gets, then you'll remember the scene in the doctor's office when, after his session with the therapist, as he is walking out the door, Jack's character turns around to see the room filled with other patients, all waiting for their turn for therapy. Jack's character says, "Is this as good as it gets?"

This question can translate into our lives, too. Look around at your life, the achievements you have made, and the ones you haven't. Are there any areas of your life you think you cannot get any better at? If this really is as good as the situation is going to get, then any amount of intentional action isn't going to matter. You must be committed and ready to make it better, no matter the struggle.

You could be dealing with a physical or mental handicap, or a block in your self-esteem may be holding you back. Is it fear? Or, the belief that this is just the way life is, and this is the hand you were dealt? We are all dealing with our own struggles. It might seem your situation is unique, but there are people out there going through similar struggles, and many of them are worse off.

The question Jack Nicholson's character was asking was essentially, "Is change possible, or is this it? Am I destined to live a life of chaos and uncertainty?"

Our limitations are, for the most part, decided by many factors. Most limits we hold onto are mired in old beliefs. This impacts our "deliberate practice model". This is when we ask ourselves, "How can I act if there is the high chance I will fail? Do I have what it takes? Am I talented enough?"

Let me tell you something about success and talent. It is 90% work. You need to stop mucking around with your time and focus on what matters. I look around, and I see a world losing ground every day, wrapped up in all the massive amounts of information and media outlets that pull us into the arena of negativity and false lies.

You should set up your beliefs to carry you forward, not hold you back. The path of an Undefeated warrior is best lived when they determine the intentional actions needed to reach the outcome visualized by following a detailed plan.

Make a firm decision about what you want to accomplish, the values you choose to live by, and the principles that will guide you where you need to be. Finally, focus all your attention on achieving whatever would have the greatest impact on what matters most to you.

In the end, how good it gets is up to you.

Focus.

Intention.

Accountability.

Firm decisions.

Consistent improvement.

All this is yours, if you want it.

"We like to think of our **champions** and idols as superheroes who were born different from us. We don't like to think of them as relatively **ordinary people** who made themselves **extraordinary**."

— **Carol Dweck,** bestselling author of *Mindset*

The Unbeatable Mindset: "I Can Do This!"

"Believe in yourself! Have faith in your abilities! Without a humble but reasonable confidence in your own powers, you cannot be successful or happy."

— Norman Vincent Peale

Your mindset, and the attitude you choose to adopt and develop, are very powerful tools. In fact, without the right mindset, all the other strategies and sound advice I have discussed in this book up until now have no foundation to build themselves on.

Most people who give up have adopted the mindset that they are not worthy of finishing what they started. They don't believe in their purpose, and so, when confronted with difficult obstacles, they run. Or, they do nothing. Their first thought is, "I can't deal with this," or "It isn't supposed to be this hard, right?"

However, it is hard. It is hard to stand resilient, filled with grit and determination, committed to keep going until the end, breaking through barrier after barrier... folks, this is the way. There are no shortcuts. If there were, this book would be 10 pages long, and you'd be sitting on a beach in Maui, reflecting on your success.

In this chapter, I will give you the strategies to develop an unbeatable mindset that can go up against anything and win. Will you conquer or be conquered? Will you say, "I can!"—no matter what? Or, will you groan about how unfair life is and say you never asked for any of this? It's up to you. It has always been up to you— even when it seemed like someone else was directing your destiny.

You have been—and always will be—the masterful creator of everything you reap and sow.

Your mindset is your own.

As Viktor Frankl said, *"Everything can be taken from a man but one thing, the last of human freedoms: To choose one's attitude in any given set of circumstances, to choose one's own way."*

People who can, believe they can. People who don't or won't—even if they want it—will never get what they desire, because they don't believe. You must believe you can, or else you won't.

Your **mindset is a choice.**

We are conditioned to believe we can't do certain things in life. This is true of creative arts, music, sports, or academics. How often do you say to yourself or people, "I can't..." and then fill in the blank? Yes, there are many things we can't do... yet. For example, I have always dreamed of playing the piano, but when I was growing up, I never pursued this hidden passion, and it stayed buried inside me for 40 years. Why?

Conditioned limitations. Someone once told me I had no musical talent. Those words stuck with me, and I stayed away from anything that was musical. I believed it at the time. When someone asked if I played something, I said, "No, I'm not very good at music." However, that wasn't true. I believe I was good at music. I would write songs, even without knowing the notes. I'd come up with lyrics and pass them on to other musicians.

By telling people you can't do something, it reinforces your failure. What you say is what you do. Growing up, I defeated myself continuously by reinforcing the belief that "I can't."

However, it didn't end there. This attitude started trickling into other areas of my life, as well. Soon, I convinced myself I couldn't do Grade-10 math. So, I ended up failing it twice. My mind was set on what I could and couldn't do. I had set my limits, and every action taken was designed to work within those limited parameters.

This is how people remain defeated, day in and day out. We tell ourselves we can't, or we shouldn't. We believe in our limitations, as if they define us. Limitations are built on past failures or shortcomings, and over time, your limits define who you are. It's sad but true. This goes for everything: The amount of money you make; the work you do; the people you hang out with; and the way you spend your time.

What do you do when you are alone and nobody else is watching? You are defining your destiny through the actions you take.

Your world is a mirrored reflection of the mindset you have developed. Circumstances have nothing to do with it. The fact that you had a tough childhood, or you were treated poorly by your teachers throughout school, or your parents neglected you, has nothing to do with who you ultimately decide to be.

Choose, and it is yours. Let others make that decision, and you give up your freedom to create, experiment, and experience.

Whether you were born on this side of town or another, or you had to work 12 hours a day just to make ends meet, this has nothing to do with where you are today. If you want to predict your future, take a step back, and then, step into your own mindset. It is the cornerstone of your success or failure.

Ask yourself these questions:

- Do you complain about your situation and wish it were different?

- Do you put the blame on someone else for making you unhappy?

- Do you see yourself as a victim, trapped in an impossible world with no chance of escape?

If you answered "yes" to at least one of these questions, now the healing begins. Believing in your limitations gives them power over you. By reinforcing this victim mindset, you are painting yourself into a corner of limited possibilities. The other side of the fence is a world full of unlimited potential.

In fact, it only takes one limiting belief to corrupt your success in life. One negative belief about who you are, your abilities, and what is possible for you, can carve out a lifetime of living within the confines of limited potential and wretched poverty.

I am talking about poverty of the mind, in which you become so poor intellectually that you never really make any progress in your life. You are so poor in positive thinking and stuck in your past failures and dreams that never came true, you face defeat every day... and feel powerless to do anything about it.

If you feel trapped, helpless, limited, or poor, it is because you're living your life from the perspective of a fixed mindset. If you're trapped, you can get unstuck. You can walk out of that place. Are you certain you can't do something? You most likely can, when you switch from a fixed to a growth mindset.

In Carol S. Dweck's bestselling book, *Mindset*, she discussed the fixed and growth mindset:

> "In a fixed mindset, people believe their qualities are fixed traits and therefore cannot change. ... According to Dweck, when a student has a fixed mindset, they believe that their basic abilities, intelligence, and talents are fixed traits. They think that you are born with a certain amount and that's all you have."

Imagine what you will be able to do when you stop saying, "I can't," and begin to say, "Yes, I can!" Just repeating these words empowers your mind to believe them.

Do you think you can't find a partner to love you and spend time with you? Yes, you can!

Do you think you can't write a book because writing was never your strong point? Yes, you can write a book!

Do you think you can't earn a million dollars this year because you never finished college? Yes, you can earn a million, if you drive your actions forward.

Do you think you can't change your life because this is the way things are, and now, you have to live with it? Lies. Not true. Yes, you can change anything about your life, starting today.

Yes, you can!

Do you know what happens when you set your own limits? You create a mindset of expectations. "I expect to be this way, and so I am. I expect to earn this much, or I can expect to be working in this job 10 years from now—even though I hate it." Yes, your expectations for the future are what fix you to the outcomes. You can predict your life and how it is going to be for the next 20 years by taking a serious look at how you are living now.

By buying into your fixed mindset, and the mindset of "I can't," you are sealing your own fate. You are determining your own worth. You are setting the future in stone. You are choosing to be less-than, instead of more-than. The fixed mindset revokes challenges and takes the easy way out. It is focused on existing in a realm of comfort, while avoiding difficulties.

Let me share an example. I floundered and struggled throughout all my school years. I never had a score that was above 70, and if I did get an average score that high, it was usually in English class, where I excelled. However, most of my grades were mediocre, and I often failed classes. If there were any student more deserving of the "Most Likely to Fail at Life" award, I was the top contender.

I couldn't break free of the "D" club, which was what they called the kids who never displayed any academic ability. The teachers knew I was the lowest in the class. In fact, one of them called me "C Scotty"—meaning that I couldn't get anything above a C. That stuck with me for years, and the fixed mindset was fixed, all right.

I learned at an early age how to defeat myself in just about every area of my life. I was committed on a subconscious level to living up to what others expected of me.

What did they expect? Not very much. I delivered on that every time.

Then, one day, a teacher I never had before handed me back a paper I scored a D on. I wasn't surprised by the score at all. After all, that is what I studied for. I always put in just enough effort to scrape by.

This teacher looked at me and said, "I know you can do better." When I got the next test mark back, it was a bit higher, but I was still shooting for mediocrity. He took me aside and said, "Are you done messing around? I want a B on your next one." At this point, something shifted inside. I realized, for the first time in most of my school life, I could get that score.

Now, a B isn't exactly shooting for the dean's list, but you have to understand; I had been a D student my whole life. One day, I just decided I wasn't going to excel at anything, and nobody had ever challenged me. I had given up. I was barely holding on. Nobody cared. Feeling beaten and defeated, when I hit the mat, I stayed down.

Now, just to bring this to your attention, to varying degrees, we all have our mindset fixed on something. You can believe strongly in one ability but limit yourself in other areas.

Your goal is to stretch yourself—even if it is just a small amount—so that you move closer to developing your growth mindset. It is there, waiting for you to do something. In fact, the human mind and body were designed to grow and thrive. Your mind and body don't want to remain dormant and lazy, waiting for the day when you decide to finally do something. They want to explore, grow, and be driven to the boundaries of unlimited potential.

You, my friend, are an explorer. We were not designed to stay behind a desk, lowering ourselves to standards set by others, but I see it every day. I see the pain people are in when they know inside themselves that they are worth something more than what they buy into.

Reality check: Are you buying into someone else's version of reality? Is your environment fashioned to serve someone else's higher agenda? Are you defining what is possible, or is someone else defining this for you?

Most of my life, I said, "I can't." Your actions, beliefs, thoughts, and complete mindset are impacted by this one statement.

One day, after a series of ups and downs, addictions, and struggling with depression, when I had enough of suffering, I stopped saying, "I can't." I became a "can" person. Then, I moved up to an "I can definitely do this" person. Attitude changes everything. A negative attitude kills your future. I'll cut to the chase by saying this: Nothing that happened to you in the past matters, as far as today is concerned.

You are standing on **the edge of greatness**. You are that greatness.

How is that for thinking highly of yourself? From now on, from today, from this moment, you can.

Now, here are two areas you can develop to live the "I can" mindset.

1. Put an end to your "I can't" psychology.

Here is what you should do: Take a count of how many times a day you refuse to do or accept anything because you say, "I can't do that." It is a habit we acquired at some point in the past, when we lost confidence in our real selves. It may have evolved in school, such as, "I can't do math," or "I can't play basketball." Now, maybe you really do suck at these things. Not everyone can play basketball—no matter how hard they try—but whether you can or can't, it doesn't matter.

By building this phrase into your mindset, you start using it for everything that is challenging. In fact, saying, "I can't do something" becomes an easy cop-out. Before you know it, you are using it not just for what you can't do, but what you don't want to do. It becomes your default response.

Use "I can" when you feel you are about to resist something. For years, they were so many things I said I couldn't do, but I didn't want to do them because learning a new skill takes time and effort—two things I wasn't willing to invest.

Here are a few examples:

- "I can't cook." Well cooking isn't that difficult. I wasn't making gourmet meals, but I could cook basic food.

- "I can't save money." True, this was always challenging for me, but saving became easier when I switched my habit of spending to saving instead. Learning to invest and scale up is something I was never good at, but over time, I learned to save bigtime. In fact, I saved myself out of debt. Anyone can save cash if they learn a few basic skills and implement new saving habits.

- "I can't quit my day job." As it turns out, I could. I was just refusing to give it up because I was afraid of what would happen. When I realized that yes, I can quit this job and get something better, I took the necessary steps and made it happen.

Not being able to do something and convincing yourself you can't are two different things. 'I can't' is a limiting function that steals your life away over time. I can't always defeats you before you attempt anything, and it keeps you scared because you never rise to the challenge.

Now, you know you can, and you will. The more focused your I can power becomes, the bigger your confidence will grow.

Do you think Muhammad Ali could have come back if he had convinced himself "I can't"? He believed he could, and he did.

Would J.K. Rowling have been able to write that first Harry Potter book while she was living on welfare and caring for a child if she thought, "I can't"? She believed in her story, and Harry Potter and the Sorcerer's Stone was published in June of 1997.

Could Oprah have become the #1 TV talk show talent if she had said, "I can't do this" after being fired from a Baltimore TV station? She believed she could, and so she went on to become one of the most influential persons in the entertainment industry.

2. Use 'I can' body language.

Body language is powerful. Just look at Tony Robbins live onstage at one of his events. The man is packed with energy, and he gets everyone else moving in sync with his movements. Why? Moving your body in powerful, positive movements is immediately empowering.

You can start to recognize some of the negative messages you send about yourself just by observing your own body language. We know by controlling the way we move; we can regulate our emotions.

Confidence is more than just the way you think about yourself; that's only part of it. Strong confidence is the positive outcome you experience when you move your body in empowering ways. If you act confidently, you'll feel more vibrant and empowered.

Your body language includes hand positioning, stance, and facial expressions. This is nonverbal communication that tells a story about your level of confidence and self-esteem. Those who are highly tuned-in may be able to tell what you are feeling now.

Weak postures that communicate low self-esteem and fear are:

- Folding your arms (defensive and protective);

- Touching your face/neck (appearing nervous or uncomfortable);

- Hands in pockets;

- Keeping your distance;

- Eyes downcast or off to the side (lacking confidence and expressing shame); and

- Low tone and unclear voice (lacking confidence and expressing fear of saying the wrong thing).

Any kind of body language that is stripping away our confidence and making us standoffish should be changed to portray someone who is honest, open, and, best of all, not easy to defeat.

Once again, you communicate your sense of worth to the world when you use your body in ways most people just never take advantage of. Many people are too careful not to draw attention to themselves. They don't want to look silly or stand out as the odd one in a crowd.

Well, it never stopped world-class comedian Jim Carrey, who has made over 40 films and brought joy to millions of movie-goers through his animated facial and body language. I know; you are not Jim Carrey—and you don't have to be—but get creative with the body language you use to make people laugh, feel joy, or get inspired.

There are too many people out there, walking around with their heads down, not smiling, hands in their pockets, saying to the world, "Look, I've been defeated by life."

You are not defeated by life; you can only be beaten by acting that way.

Start with a smile. Smiling can change everything for you in an instant. It reduces stress, and it's a positive form of communication. People see that, and they want to talk to you, be your friend, and open their doors to you. Smiling brings opportunity. It conveys you're not only happy, but you are a person who feels good about themselves.

Here's what you can do:

1. In the morning, work on smiling for 10 minutes. Make it a morning exercise, just like any other exercise routine.

2. Smile when you're around your children or other loved ones. Let them know it's important.

Imitate the people who move with confidence, assurance, and positive body language. Watch how they react and express their emotions. By imitating others, we can attain similar results, and eventually, find our own style of communicating.

"Defeat brings a lesson; it gives a chance to **rebuild**, a chance to start again with the **knowledge** of what does not work."

— Leon Brown

Building Your Undefeated Lifestyle

"The common denominator of success—the secret of success of every man who has ever been successful—lies in the fact that he formed the habit of doing things that failures don't like to do."

— Albert E.N. Gray

It's game time. We have come to the end of Undefeated, and now I'm confident you have everything needed to put into practice and make yourself unstoppable. This is the time when the rubber meets the road, and you take full responsibility for everything that happens to your future from here on out.

Don't sweat it, you've got this covered.

To get ahead, you have to think ahead. To be the best and be on top of your game, you have to be willing to do things other people aren't doing. When others are fearful of the future and too paralyzed to move, you'll be charging ahead towards the finish line. When someone makes an excuse for why it can't be done, you will be showing them how to do it.

You are going to commit to taking action toward four principles to gain total clarity on developing an Undefeated lifestyle. This journey is a never-ending trip. You will never stop learning, taking intentional action and becoming the best version of yourself.

First, learn what you must. Then, apply the principles you learn to make life better for you, your friends and family, and the people you have the opportunity to impact. Finally, share your knowledge with those who are willing to listen and learn. You have the power to help others move from "helpless and defeated" to Undefeated.

Principle 1: Be Willing to Do Whatever it Takes to Succeed

Will you determine what your one big thing is and then commit? Are you ready to face the adversity and be willing to do what it takes to get there? Can you feel the fear but you're ready to take intentional action anyway?

If so, I commend you for this. It takes courage and guts to commit to something that has no guarantee of success. Isn't that the one thing that holds most people back?

They don't want to do something, unless they have a solid guarantee it's going to work out for them. They won't make a move, unless someone can convince them this investment of time, money, or energy is the best path to take.

While I can't guarantee you success, one thing is for sure: If you follow the program here, you will have a 90% advantage over the rest of the people out there without a plan. Too many people are settling for the sure bet that rarely comes along.

An artist works for years on a painting, never really knowing if anybody will give it a second glance. An author spends a year or more writing a book, never knowing if a publisher will publish it. An athlete practices for hours a day for a year, without knowing if they will make the team.

If you are looking for a guarantee, there is only one way to guarantee something: Do nothing. Just do what you have always done, and you will get what you have always gotten. If you take no chances, work on nothing, and have no plan, I can guarantee your situation will not change.

So, this brings us to the game plan of the Undefeated. In this book, we have already covered the essential traits people who win at life possess. They are resilient, persistent fighters. They have learned to give up is to lose, and to lose is to return to the table of defeat. If you have fight left in you, you can always take one more go at it.

During a big loss, how do we get back up and stay up? What keeps us going? Is there a skill we haven't looked at yet that we can add to the success freedom formula?

If you want to climb a mountain, you need to ask yourself, what training is required for me to climb that mountain? What equipment do I need? Can I use the equipment I have, or will it fail me when it comes time to climb? How much time should I commit to training for the climb before I am ready?

We all have our own mountains to climb in this life, but it isn't the size of the mountain that defeats us. It is our level of belief, our commitment to the task. Do you look at the mountain and see it as some insurmountable obstacle? Or, do you see it as a challenge you are willing to take on?

Willingness is one of the core principles of an Undefeated mindset. If we are not willing, we will only talk about the things that interest us. Are you just interested in winning? Or, are you ready to take the necessary action right now to push past your resistance? Do you believe without a doubt that this thing is yours to achieve? Or, are you willing to accept defeat if beaten? If you do fall off the mountain, will you try to climb it again from a new angle? Or, will you walk away, done with the fight?

These questions can be applied to any challenge in your life. Before you do something, ask yourself if it is going to have the impact you want or need. Will it be a benefit, or will it have a negative impact? For example, let's say, you are trying to lose weight and gain muscle because your goal is to participate in a triathlon. Yet, you are struggling to resist the temptation to eat donuts at work.

Now, one donut might not kill you, but if this action of giving in is reinforced when you feel it pulling on you, your reaction will be to eat junk. You'll keep the weight on and hate yourself for doing it. You know what you should have done was say "no," but instead, your weaker self just stepped in and tried to indulge one last time.

By choosing one path, you reject another. By saying "yes" to another donut, you are saying "no" to losing weight, or winning a competition. By saying "yes" to polluting your body with other bad junk—such as excessive alcohol, smoking, junk food, or stress—you are subconsciously making a choice to live a life of poor quality.

You must be willing to make your choices, and then, you must be willing to accept responsibility for them. Ever been around someone who complains all the time? Exhausting, isn't it? That person is undoubtedly blaming someone—or everyone—for the way things turned out.

Remember, when this happens, we turn ourselves into helpless victims. Helpless victims never find a way out of their pain. They are wrapped in it. They are defeated by everything around them, but, worst of all, they are defeated by themselves.

When we lack the willpower to say "no"—even when it goes against our personal promises—this is a form of self-defeat. So, how do we stay in tune with what really matters? How do we defeat ourselves, before anyone else has the chance to do so?

The mindset of an Undefeated person—and one of the most critical principles—is holding themselves accountable. Nobody is responsible for your life, success, or happiness more than you are. Nothing can break you, until you choose to break yourself.

Nothing can defeat your resilience, until you give up under the pressure of a stronger opponent. Nobody can drag you down, unless you allow them to. Stop looking for the source of strength outside yourself. You won't find it in other people, sugary drinks, drugs, or any other form of addictions.

The only thing that makes you strong—and, ultimately, undefeatable—is a commitment to an unbreakable resolve. Where do you find this resolve? How do we tap into this source of power when we hit the mat, and it looks like defeat is inevitable? At what point should we give in?

This brings me to the second principle of a person who remains Undefeated.

Principle 2: Make Your Decision—Form the Habits Most Are Unwilling to Form

In looking at the habits and behaviors of super-resilient people who pushed through and persevered, there is one dominating trait they all share: It is a commitment to doing whatever it takes to win. In other words, they do what 98% of the population wouldn't do. Going the distance isn't just finishing the race but taking it the extra mile.

Be the one who goes the extra round. The author who writes just one more book after the previous five have failed. The entrepreneur who takes a chance on one more business opportunity with the last dollar they have. The runner who pushes the last mile when most have stopped.

When most people are still sleeping, you are up at 5 AM, putting yourself to the test. Your mind is in the game, and you're clear on your goals. If you want to win, you have to have a winning mindset. This means staying true to your mission and purpose.

Model the successful people you love and respect. Achievements aside, what traits of the people whose mission you're following do you want to emulate? What do they do that sets them apart from everyone else?

Throughout this book, I have given you plenty of stories to draw courage from. You can see the people who made their dreams come true by sticking to the course and refusing to give up, no matter the odds stacked against them.

Albert Gray—once a well-known speaker about life insurance—wrote a piece he called The Common Denominator of Success. In this paper, Albert Gray states, "The secret of success of every individual who has ever been successful lies in the fact that they formed the habit of doing things that failures don't like to do."

As he explains, people who live the life they imagined began by deciding from the get-go which habits were needed to accomplish the purpose they set out to achieve. This principle, this habit of doing things most refuse to do, is as true today as it was thousands of years ago.

You form the habits to reach the outcome, or else, your outcome will not be your own; rather, it will be the plans of someone else, who did what you could not or refused to do.

So, ask yourself: What are you willing to do that most wouldn't dare think of? When you see yourself going that extra mile, and then some, what is driving you to push beyond the edge of "just doing enough" to get by?

Let's take an example. Many people have the desire to or hope they will someday be rich, and they will have so much money, they can retire early or quit their day job and finally do what they love with a nice cushion of cash underneath them.

However, for many people, that day never comes. They never save money or build that cushion, so they never feel brave enough to take the leap. Instead, they hold onto the dream that someday, it will happen—while enjoying the lavish lifestyle of shopping whenever they want, eating at expensive restaurants, and buying a $5

Frappuccino almost daily. Do you know what a $5 latte costs over the course of a year, if you drink it every day? Do the math, and you'll see where your money is going.

Now, someone who truly wants to achieve financial success, so they can quit their crappy day job, would do what most wouldn't. This requires a plan built on taking consistent action every day. You have to want it so badly that failure is not an option. How could anyone be defeated when they are totally committed to a single course of action?

The course is not an easy one, and that is why so few engage in it, but you are here now, reading this passage and saying to yourself, "Yes, I can do what most are refusing to do, so I can have this." This could be something as simple as waking up 30 minutes earlier or saving a few extra dollars a day. You get to decide what must be done, and then, set out to do it consistently.

> "The woods are lovely dark and deep, but I have promises to keep, and miles to go before I sleep, and miles to go before I sleep."
>
> — Robert Frost

Principle 3: Focus on 1% Development Strategies

Did you know that by focusing on improving your performance by just 1% over the long-term could improve everything on an exponential scale? Let's take the example of Dave Brailsford, who was brought in to put the British cycling team on a new path to success. Up until that period, the team had failed for the past hundred years to win anything except one gold medal at the Olympic Games.

Brailsford used a strategy known as "the aggregation of marginal gains." This was the philosophy of searching for a tiny area of improvement in your habits, actions, and goals.

He proved by improving one thing by just 1% over the course of time, you can make significant gains. What look like minuscule changes are massive changes over the course of a year. The British cyclists went on to win close to 180 medals within a decade.

Don't fixate on the big changes overnight. What can you do today that would create massive change in a decade? What small habits would give you that massive edge?

Now that you have the three principles to develop your undefeatable lifestyle, how will you put these principles into practice? What can you do differently tomorrow that you have been avoiding for the past decade?

You don't have to change everything in an instant. Just by making your 1% shift and doing the "hard thing" many would not do; you raise the stakes of your inner game. Some people may look at you and question, "Why is she acting that way?" or "How come you work so hard and seem so intense?"

Intensity is the outcome of a focused mind. Get focused and stay fixed on your one thing.

Principle 4: Build the Influence of a Support Network

Did you know your success is largely dependent on the people whom you spend the most time with?

For years, I surrounded myself with the wrong people. By "wrong," I don't mean these people were bad in any sense (well, most of them, anyway) but, they didn't contribute to my well-being or quality of life, either—or perhaps, I didn't contribute to theirs.

The environment you forge, the people you forge alliances with, and the personality and quality of mindset you create with your company, all have a massive impact on the path you are living today. You might be thinking, "Everything that has happened to me so far has been by chance or destiny."

Well, maybe it has, but you are creating those chances and designing that destiny right now, at this moment. You can choose who is going to walk with you on this journey. Some people are just along for the ride; others want to help you win the race.

Forging Alliances

Everyone plays a role in each other's lives, and instead of just going with the flow of each person you interact with, you have to analyze, think, and govern the situation so that you don't let it drag you into something that could have a negative impact. Forge the wrong relationships, and you will set yourself up for failure.

What you need to do is forge an alliance with people who are working toward a similar goal—preferably, a common goal, so you can support and encourage each other. These don't have to be your friends. Don't limit yourself to just the people you know; chances are, they aren't part of the alliance you want to create.

Alliances and Partnerships That Made History

Steve Jobs partnered with Steve Wozniak and founded Apple, launching the Apple I and II. While Jobs took care of the marketing, Wozniak crushed the invention of the products.

Henry Ford partnered with James J. Couzens, and it saved the company from possibly going bankrupt. While Ford was a perfectionist and paid scrutinizing attention to the craftsmanship of the automobile, he failed to meet deadlines and would stall for months without shipping any cars. It was James J. Couzens who focused on the business side of things and convinced Ford, "Either we ship these cars or go bankrupt."

They shipped the cars.

Famed puppeteer and Muppets creator, Jim Henson partnered with Frank Oz to create some of the most memorable characters still in "show biz" today. The two had a partnership for 27 years, until Henson's untimely death in 1990.

Have you ever heard of that Internet thing called "Google"? Larry Page met Sergey Brin, and they founded the world's largest search engine, and the most successful dot-com business in history.

Legendary filmmakers, Steven Spielberg and George Lucas, teamed up in the early '70s after showing admiration for each other's fieldwork. Then, they partnered up—both onscreen and off—and collaborated to bring moviegoers the Indiana Jones series.

In 1934, Bill Hewlett and David Packard forged a relationship that eventually led to the Hewlett-Packard company, which today is worth an estimated $104.3B in annual sales.

Driven by Common Goals

Partnerships. Relationships. Driven by a common goal with clear-cut objectives to reach a seemingly impossible outcome if attempted alone. Whatever you are aiming for, seek those people who are ready to reach out and help you.

The relationships you forge with others who become part of your alliance may last for a few years (such as Jobs and Wozniak) or three decades (such as Henson and Oz), but one thing is certain: Nobody can do it alone.

People need other people to make it to the finish line. You won't cross it on your own if you keep stumbling, because when you do, your partners and trusted allies will be there to carry you across. Find those people whom you can make powerful partnerships with, be clear about your aim, and work out a strategy that builds your business and your brand and adds value to people's lives.

Just look at any company or success story, and you'll see a team of people who contributed to the overall success.

Takeaway Action Plan

1. Be clear about what your plan is. If you have a strategy, write it down.

2. Join a mastermind group that supports each other's ideas and goals. Even though you may not find that perfect "partner" to work with, just being in touch with others and sharing your ideas is going to open doors.

3. Find an accountability partner. This is someone who keeps you focused, organized, and moving toward your goal. You don't necessarily have to have the same objective, but the person should hold you accountable for deadlines and getting the work done.

4. Be clear about your objectives and mission. If you don't know what you want, you'll attract like-minded people, an alliance of individuals who don't know what they want. Do you just want your ship to sail endlessly, or do you want it to reach a specific destination? Your team will help you get there, but they can't help you if you have no map. Be clear about what you want. Be clear about whom you want to help you get there.

You need people in your corner to help. I don't care who you are; you need that one person in your corner who keeps you on your feet when you're staggering and losing the fight. You need someone there. For some people, it is their loved ones who support them through their toughest moments. This could also be a group or mastermind community you belong to.

Discover Your Team of Undefeatable Champions

Your team of undefeatable champions is going to prove themselves invaluable when the time comes. When it comes to discovering this tribe of undefeatable people, you need to know whom you want on your side. What values or characteristics do these people have? How are you going to support each other through some of life's biggest challenges?

When you know the type of people you desire to connect with, they will appear. Not knowing means you could meet someone who would be a perfect fit for your organization, and yet miss them completely.

As you move through your life as an Undefeated champion, remember it isn't about winning or losing. Just because you win a lot doesn't mean you'll never be defeated in life, and just because you lose a lot doesn't mean you'll never win.

Belonging to the Undefeated isn't about results or a scorecard. It is about the champion heart and mindset. It isn't talent, but determination, and it isn't about winning, but showing up again and again to keep doing what you do best. This is how mastery is practiced. Mastery isn't perfection, but practice. It isn't how you win the game, but how you play the game.

We all lose at times, and, in most cases, we lose more than we win. So, to be a winner, you need a winning mindset.

A winning mindset is deciding you are here to do what you do best and to do it better than anyone else, and if someone does it better than you, learn from that person, so you can level up your life in whatever venture you pursue.

Don't give up because someone else tells you the game is over. It is over when you decide to throw in the towel, and if you do, that is okay, because maybe you just need to find another way to do something. What doesn't work one way could work in another.

I want you to pursue all the things in your life that matter. You decide your wins and losses. You choose the path that fits your ambition. What drives you is what you should pay attention to.

I wish you all the best on your continuing journey. Keep pushing forward, keep going, and keep up the good fight.

I leave you now with a quote I live by every day:

> "If you have a strong mind and plant in it a firm resolve, you can change your destiny."
>
> — Paramahansa Yogananda

Take charge of your destiny.

Go and build your thing.

Make it count.

I'll see you on the other side of *Undefeated*.

Scott Allan

"Stay **true** to yourself, yet always be open to learn. **Work hard** and never give up on your **dreams**— even when nobody else believes they can come true but you. These are not clichés but real tools you need—no matter what you do in life—to stay **focused** on your path."

— Phillip Sweet

About Scott Allan

Scott Allan is a bestselling author who has a passion for teaching, building life skills, and inspiring others to take charge of their lives.

Scott's mission is to give people the strategies needed to design the life they want through choice.

He believes successful living is a series of small, consistent actions taken every day to build a thriving lifestyle with intentional purpose.

By taking the necessary steps and eliminating unwanted distractions that keep you stuck, you are free to focus on the essentials.

You can connect with Scott online:

Instagram

https://www.instagram.com/scottallanauthor/

Facebook

https://www.facebook.com/scottallanauthor

What Did You Think of Undefeated?

First of all, thank you for purchasing this book <u>Undefeated</u>. I know you could have picked any number of books to read, but you picked this book and for that I am extremely grateful.

If you enjoyed this book and found some benefit in reading this, I'd like to hear from you and hope that you could take some time to <u>post a review on Amazon</u>.

Your feedback and support will help this author to greatly improve his writing craft for future projects and make this book even better.

All the best,

Scott Allan

Printed in Great Britain
by Amazon

69460060R00121